The Race to Reach Out

The Race to Reach Out

CONNECTING NEWCOMERS TO CHRIST IN A NEW CENTURY

DOUGLAS T. ANDERSON
MICHAEL J. COYNER

Abingdon Press
Nashville

THE RACE TO REACH OUT:
CONNECTING NEWCOMERS TO CHRIST IN A NEW CENTURY

This book is printed on acid-free paper.

Library of Congress Cataloging-in-Publication Data

Anderson, Douglas T., 1951-
 The race to reach out : connecting newcomers to Christ in a new century / Douglas T. Anderson and Michael J. Coyner.
    p.   cm.
 Includes bibliographical references.
 ISBN 0-687-06668-9 (binding: pbk. : alk. paper)
 1. Church growth. 2. Church work with new church members. I. Coyner, Michael J. II. Title.
 BV652.25.A535 2004
 254'.5—dc22

                                                                    2004005979

04 05 06 07 08 09 10 11 12 13—10 9 8 7 6 5 4 3 2 1

MANUFACTURED IN THE UNITED STATES OF AMERICA

To our wives, Jan and Marsha,
our families,
Lyle Schaller (our longtime mentor),
and to those who welcome newcomers
into the life of the church

Contents

Introduction: Teamwork is the Key

Running on the track team during my senior year of high school taught me a lot about teamwork. I enjoyed running and loved to compete in track, but I was not the fastest individual runner. My track coach made me a relay specialist. This stroke of genius appealed to my competitive nature; I was not simply a third- or fourth-place runner in individual events, but rather a relay specialist. I could make a difference for the team. I had something to offer. I could help us win.

So I worked very hard in my new role. I worked on my speed, endurance, conditioning, and running curves smoothly and evenly—just like the rest of the team. But I worked especially hard on the handoffs. I worked on precise timing so the baton would be exchanged smoothly and efficiently within the exchange zone, which was absolutely essential to avoid disqualification.

Those lessons proved to be valuable not only on the track, they also become a central metaphor for my understanding of ministry. I came to realize that many aspects of ministry require a teamwork that is similar to running a relay race in a track meet. This is especially true for the process of assimilating newcomers.

First, assimilating new disciples is a team effort. Newcomer assimilation should never be a solo event that the pastor does for the congregation. The pastor is not the solo runner with the congregation on the sideline, either cheering the pastor's success or criticizing when the results are less than hoped for or expected. Assimilation is a team process, a team ministry—as God intends it to be.

Second, speed is important. Quickly responding to newcomers when they visit our church the first time is critical. When we hold back in order not to appear "pushy" or manipulative, most newcomers will view this as indifference or coldness. Working to improve our speed is not only essential in a race, it is also imperative in our follow-up of newcomers.

Third, timing matters as we connect with newcomers in a timely manner to help them move through the process of assimilation and discipleship from one step to the next. Speed counts, but only when it is partnered with timing.

Fourth, running the turns is another key to success. Skillful runners learn to lean into the turns, and not fight them in order to maintain momentum and balance. The same is important in assimilating new disciples. The assimilation process needs to be flexible and adaptable enough to take changes of direction in stride, anticipating them and adjusting to them.

Fifth, handoffs are critical. Being able to exchange the baton smoothly and efficiently is a primary, required skill in running a relay race well. The church also must be able to make a smooth "handoff" of care, contact, and vital information about the needs, interests, gifts, talents, and passions of the newcomer so that he or she can be vitally connected to God and others.

And sixth, constant practice is essential. A good relay team works constantly on the skills necessary to be victorious, and effective newcomer assimilation teams do the same. They stay in contact with newcomers consistently, and they evaluate their process in order to improve their effectiveness in connecting people to Jesus Christ and to his Church.

In the following chapters, you will be introduced to newcomers, and you will follow them as they are assimilated in discipleship. You will also see the workings of the Newcomers Team who strive to help those newcomers be assimilated. The analogy of the relay race will provide the background for this story, and you will also learn the practical reasons for each lap of the race. So now that you see the crucial race of newcomer assimilation that we plan to run together in this book, there is really only one more thing to be said in preparation:

Runners, take your marks, get set, and let's go!

Douglas T. Anderson
Muncie, Indiana

What is the
Motivation?

A passion for running (and winning) was the motivation for Doug's relay race. What is the passion that might lead a pastor and a church to take seriously the issues involved in assimilating new disciples? Attracting newcomers, welcoming them, keeping track of their involvement, hearing their concerns and needs, inviting them to belong, and mentoring them into full discipleship—all of that is hard work. Churches and pastors who want to enter into this ministry should begin by examining their motivation.

One motivation that will fail is the motivation of institutional survival. We are not advocating that you focus upon assimilating new disciples because of any simple desire to keep your church alive, to meet denominational membership goals, or to have a sense of your own success in ministry.

No, the only adequate motivation for assimilating new disciples is *a passion for God and a passion for people*. First, you have to believe that God makes a difference in people's lives and that people without God as a focus in their lives are lost, searching, and empty. Without this passion for God, no church can continue to focus upon the hard work of assimilating new disciples.

The other side of that passion is a passion for people. Ministry is about people, it is about caring for people, and it is about a yearning for all people to discover what it means to be a disciple of Christ in their journey toward God. Entering fully into a ministry of assimilating new disciples means that you care for those newcomers, you eagerly desire to see their lives find fulfillment, you are willing to adapt your church's ministry to meet their needs, and you are willing to be an advocate for those new disciples.

We live in an age when those outside the church are checking our integrity as a church. If newcomers notice that we are only interested in adding members, or if they get a sense that we only want them to fit our needs as a church, then those newcomers will disappear in a hurry. Likewise if we as a church start to welcome such newcomers, but then fail to follow through and actually include them, they will leave us very disillusioned about the church (and perhaps the faith). This ministry of assimilating new disciples is serious—and joyous—ministry. It is not something to be taken lightly, and it is not something to be started if we do not intend to complete the race.

And so I admonish you, before you run this race, check your motivation. Ask yourself why you want to help assimilate new disciples. See if you have the passion to start and to finish the race. Then you will be ready for this ministry and for this book, and you will indeed hear our words: Runners, take your marks, get set, and let's go!

Michael J. Coyner
Fargo, North Dakota

CHAPTER ONE

Attracting Newcomers

B ill and Cathy Johnson approached the entrance to First Church with some trepidation. Even though they had been very involved in church in their previous community, the Middleton Church was much smaller than this large downtown campus at First Church. And of course this was yet one more transition during a busy summer of their lives, which included moving to the city with Bill's job transfer, buying a new home, getting used to new neighbors, new shopping centers, new doctors and dentists and car mechanics. Just thinking about all of that made Cathy feel anxious all over again. She quickly told herself, "Come on, you are in your midfifties and you have grown children. You can do this."

She and Bill had decided to try attending First Church after a whole series of events. First came the job transfer and move, then Bill found in his office several peers who were involved at First Church, and one of them even casually invited Bill and Cathy to come to the church, saying simply, "It's a great place, and I think you would enjoy it." That was nice to hear, but Bill and Cathy still spent some time getting settled in their new home for a few weeks. Finally as fall approached and they thought about all of the ways they had been so involved in their church in Middleton, they decided it was time to look for a new church home.

First they checked the Yellow Pages to see all of the different churches in the city that were a part of their denomination. They had discussed this, and they decided to start with churches of their own denomination, and then if they weren't successful, they would branch out into other familiar denominations. The ad for First Church caught their eye almost immediately. It was large, with two-color type styles, and it was the only one that included a nice map to show the church's location. Spotting that ad, Bill had said to Cathy, "That must be the same church that Sam Cotolli mentioned at the office—you know, the one I told you about. He even invited us to come sometime. He wasn't pushy or anything, but I could tell that he really enjoys his church."

That seemed to settle it, and Cathy agreed that they should go to worship at First Church the next Sunday. So here they were, after finding the church easily (the map in the Yellow Pages really helped), they quickly located a parking space, and now they found themselves walking into the large, attractive entryway. Bill started surveying the situation with the eyes of a former church trustee and thinking, "This looks like it has been recently remodeled—it is so open and airy and accessible."

Cathy was still nervous, wondering if the people on the other side of the church doors would be anything like the good friends she had found at their old church in Middleton. She was still missing those friends and she felt, once again, some of the grief of this move. "Maybe," she thought, "finding a church home will help. I sure hope they have a choir that needs another singer." Choir had been her main involvement at Middleton, and it was also the place she felt most comfortable making friends.

Bill and Cathy walked through the door of First Church for their first Sunday there.

* * *

A few minutes later, in fact a few minutes after the worship service had already started, Jennifer Rodriguez came through those same doors of First Church. "Why am I always late?" she thought. But then quickly she felt the tug of a child on each hand, and she realized, "Being a mom to these two kids always seems to make me late. Will they ever get old enough to get themselves ready on time?" Feeling the stress of getting her two children ready, on the bus, and to the church was only part of her anxiety.

Jennifer had been going through lots of changes in her life. Her marriage (which she realized now had come at too young an age) had not lasted, and now she found herself a single mother. (Gosh, she hated that term!) She loved her two kids: Maria was now six and Samuel ("Sammy" as he quickly told anyone, because his hero was Sammy Sosa) was just four. They were great kids, but her life was not easy. She was trying to go back to school to complete her degree and to make herself more employable. After all, a thirty-two-year-old single mother (there was that term again) without a college degree had very limited job options.

So now she was working as a waitress at a small café and going to school. The costs of childcare made that almost impossible, but she was getting student loans and her bosses were great people who helped out. In fact, she smiled at the thought of calling them her "bosses" at all. Phil and Carrie Larsen were like parents to her. They treated their café employees like family, and they had often helped Jennifer with childcare, with flexible working hours, and even with advances on her paycheck when she needed it. Of course Jennifer was a hard worker, and her kids were adorable, and it was obvious to the Larsens that she was really trying. But still it was wonderful for Jennifer to feel the support and care of people like Phil and Carrie. It helped to keep her going, and it helped her overcome her sense of loneliness.

Here she was, entering the doors of this large church, wondering, "How did I ever get here?" Her wondering was not just about this church and this location, it was a true question about her life and its future.

How she got to First Church was kind of surprising. She rode by it nearly every day on the bus from her apartment to the café and on to school at the community college. She had often noticed the beauty and peacefulness of that building, but it never occurred to her to consider attending. But then one day on the bus she noticed a large banner at the church announcing a divorce recovery workshop. Jennifer did not have time to attend that workshop, what with her work and school schedule, but still she noticed. She remembered thinking, "Wow, what *a great idea! A church that cares about helping people like me recover. That must be a good place."*

She did not think much more about First Church for many weeks. But this morning as the kids were watching TV and had on one of those religious channels, she had felt herself concerned for her children and their upbringing. Jennifer herself grew up Catholic, but her family never attended church much. But Jennifer's mother had made sure the kids got to religion classes when they were young, and Jennifer had even been confirmed, but never too active in church after that. Jennifer never quit believing in God, she just had never found a church or a priest or pastor who seemed to be very relevant for her life. Now, as her own children were getting old enough to learn some Bible verses and some morality, Jennifer realized that she wanted that kind of religious training for them, too.

So that Sunday morning as the kids watched the religious channel, Jennifer decided that maybe it was time to look for a church for the kids. She remembered that banner at First Church, and she looked up their phone number and called. Fortunately she got a nice recorded message that included the times of their services. Looking at her watch and seeing that it was already nine thirty, she made a spontaneous decision to try to get the kids and herself ready in time for the eleven o'clock service. They had almost made it on time, and now she rushed up to the doors of First Church, with one child in tow on each side, and she was wondering if she had made a mistake. This place was big! And it was beautiful! Did she really belong in a place like this? Would she be dressed well enough, and would her kids behave?

Jennifer was not very sure about all of this, but she and her children walked through the doors into First Church.

* * *

ATTRACTING NEWCOMERS BEGINS WITH AWARENESS

The preparation for any relay race begins long before the starter's pistol is sounded. After donning their uniforms, team members gather to begin stretching and getting their muscles ready for the upcoming race. Without proper stretching, runners risk tight muscles that can hinder performance or even cause serious injury. So stretching and reaching are not merely preparation for the race; they really are the first stage of the race.

The same thing is true when it comes to our relay race of assimilating newcomers. The church also needs to stretch gradually and intentionally, in order to reach out to newcomers so they might be connected to God's love as well. Reaching out will also cause us to stretch beyond our comfort zone toward those we may not know and toward those who are much different from us. That uncomfortable stretch is the beginning of our race of assimilating new disciples.

The stretching process of assimilation begins by attracting newcomers to come and see what is happening in the life of our church, and thereby to discover God's amazing love. That attraction might first occur through a worship service, or by attending a small-group gathering for sharing, prayer, and Bible study. Then again, their first contact might be to help in a ministry of the church, like helping with a Habitat for Humanity house or serving in a soup kitchen. All of these can be entryways into a life of the church and faith in Jesus Christ. To attract newcomers we must first make them aware that we're here, and what we're here for.

There are at least four ways in which we as church can make newcomers aware of our existence and our purpose: word of mouth, advertising, service evangelism, and invitation. Each has its own strengths, merits, and unique advantages, and each can be helpful in attracting newcomers to the church so they can be connected to God's love in Jesus Christ.

WORD OF MOUTH

One of the most helpful types of awareness that a church may have is widespread word-of-mouth communication where people in the community know about your church and its ministry even if they do not attend it or participate in its various activities. The wider the word-of-mouth awareness in the local community, the better the opportunity for attracting newcomers to that church.

Lyle Schaller once observed that churches tend to be known within the community by one of Four P's: property, pastor, people, or programs.[1] Sometimes churches are primarily known for their property—the white-frame church on the hill, the big church at the northern edge of the city, the brick church on the downtown square, or the new church that meets in the Elm Road Elementary School. So in this case, the church is primarily recognized as a building or location

In other situations, the church identified is built around the pastor of the church. The church is described within the community as Dr. Smith's church or the Reverend Jones's chapel or the place where Pastor Williams preaches. The pastor is the primary focus of the church and the point of identification for the community.

Other churches are known by the people who make up the congregation. So one church is described as being blue-collar and another as white-collar. Another congregation might be seen as where all the teachers go while another church is perceived to be the place where the community leaders attend. Of course some churches are seen as intentionally and vibrantly inclusive, with a wide variety of social classes, economic groups, and ethnic backgrounds.

Still other churches are identified by programs and ministries. One church is the home of the soup kitchen. Another church has an outstanding music ministry. This church has a widely attended and growing youth group, while that church is known throughout the area for its Bible teaching.

Lyle Schaller further observed that most churches would prefer to be known for their people and programs, especially if they want to attract and connect with newcomers. For smaller churches, it is helpful to be known by their people and the quality of caring relationships as a family of God. For larger churches, it is important to be known primarily by their programs and ministries, because those are the primary ways that larger churches attract and connect newcomers into its life and the life of

Christian faith. For midsize churches, it is difficult to compete with large churches in the quality and variety of the programs they offer (or with small churches in the quality of care and sense of family that they provide). It becomes imperative that midsize churches develop a specialty ministry that they do as well as or better than any other church in their ministry area—some specific ministry that lifts them above being simply generic (because newcomers are not attracted to generic churches). For example, one midsize church in a small community started a nursery school that served the entire community and lifted the visibility of the church and its ministry to give it broad awareness throughout the area. Word of mouth in the community said, "That is the church with the nursery school open to everyone, so they are a church that cares about children."

One word of caution: most churches have a less positive word-of-mouth awareness in their community than they expect or like to believe. If you want to know the word-of-mouth awareness of your church, ask some community people and invite them to be honest. You may not like what you hear, but it may help you to work on improving your image.

ADVERTISING AND MARKETING

Another potential means for increasing awareness of a church in its community is through advertising and marketing. Some churches have been resistant to using advertising to increase their visibility because it seems too commercial and even a bit crass. Although advertising can be used to manipulate, it can also be a wonderful tool for stretching and reaching out widely to persons we might not know personally and who may be very different from us. When it is used well, advertising is based upon a solid sense of marketing.

Such marketing goes beyond simply selling. Selling focuses on encouraging customers to buy what we have to offer; marketing focuses on learning what customers need, developing that product or service in response to those needs, and then communicating (through advertising) the availability of that product or service to meet their needs. When a church does good marketing, it first becomes aware of the needs of the people in the area it is trying to reach. That church then develops ministries and programs to meet those specific needs, especially the deep and significant spiritual needs. Then the church communicates through its advertising what it has to offer to meet the needs of persons in the community. So advertising is simply the church telling its story of what it has to offer to meet real and spiritual needs of those also hungering for wholeness.

Such advertising is not a single event but a lengthy process. Communicators say that most persons need to have a message communicated to them at least seven times in several different ways before they finally begin to recognize and understand it. It is not a quick and easy process to communicate in a way that attracts people to respond to and act on what you have communicated. Several years ago a pastoral colleague printed an attractive brochure about the church that he was serving. He and several volunteers from the church distributed that brochure to over two hundred homes in a nearby trailer park on a Saturday. The next morning he and the volunteers eagerly waited to greet and welcome the many anticipated newcomers that they expected from the trailer park as the fruit of their previous day's labor. They were instead stunned and disappointed when not one newcomer came to worship that morning. The pastor and church leaders simply were not aware that creating awareness is a process, not an event.

What they experienced is what marketers refer to as the stages of readiness.[2] To help a person move from a stage of unawareness to a stage of action is a process that requires time, patience, and creative communication. Advertising is about helping persons move through the stages of readiness. The first stage of awareness is actually unawareness, where the potential newcomer is unaware of the church and its activities and ministries. One hopes that the church's advertising will bring the newcomer to the second stage of readiness, which is awareness. At this stage the newcomer is aware that the church exists, but does not yet have an interest in the church. Continuing communication through advertising helps the newcomer move to the third stage of readiness: comprehension. At this stage the newcomer becomes familiar with some of the ministries and programs that the church has to offer but may not yet connect many of those ministries and programs to his personal and spiritual needs. So the church's advertising continues to communicate with the newcomer in order to help him develop an interest in those ministries and programs, which is the fourth stage of readiness. The newcomer sees how the church's offerings might be of interest and use to him at some point in his life, but not right now. For example, the church might advertise about an upcoming divorce recovery group that is of interest to a newly divorced person, although he or she is still not yet ready to attend. For that to occur, the newcomer must move to the fifth stage of readiness, which is a desire. Desire is a deeper connection of the newcomer's need and the church's particular program or ministry. Continuing advertising can help create such a desire in the heart of the newcomer to have his or her need met that he or she will come to the divorce recovery group. But still the newcomer will not attend until he or she reaches the sixth stage of readiness, which is action, or taking the step of attending the church or one of its ministries.

The important thing to remember about the stages of readiness and advertising is that persons must go through all six stages to arrive at readiness. This may happen almost instantaneously when people make a spur-of-the-moment decision to buy a product, or it may take several months or even years. If the communication through advertising is done periodically and consistently four to six times a year over the next few years, each time would help several persons move through the stages of readiness for action. And over time, some persons would probably move to act and attend the church. Effective church advertising that communicates well to potential newcomers is an ongoing process, not a single event.

A variety of media is available to the church in order to communicate what it has to offer in meeting real needs of potential newcomers and thereby create increased awareness of the church. Which media a church chooses will depend upon several factors, including availability, budget, size of church and community, and the group of potential newcomers that the church is attempting to reach. Larger churches in larger communities might use television or billboards effectively. Wide use of Yellow Pages and Web sites is particularly helpful for persons new to the community. In smaller communities as well as larger ones, use of direct mail such as brochures and fliers can create awareness of the church among potential newcomers with something in common, and often those types of mailings can be carefully directed to a smaller, target area. Church ads on the church page of a newspaper rarely communicate with those who are unchurched, but they tend only to inform those who already have an interest or desire and are ready to act on it.

Whatever particular medium is chosen for advertising, it is important that the information offered there is extremely user friendly, especially for those who have little or no familiarity with churches and church language. The language needs to be easily understood by unchurched persons. Churches need to check their advertisements carefully to avoid assumptions that are only understood by those inside the church. Highlight what you perceive will be important to the newcomers you are looking to attract. For younger adults with children, that will include nursery care, children's programs, parenting classes, and perhaps a divorce recovery group. For older adults, that might include accessibility, meal service, and seniors programs. Most all newcomers welcome information about air conditioning and available parking. All of this information needs to be readily available on a Sunday morning, because that is when most potential newcomers make their decision to attend worship (which is why many churches leave friendly recorded messages on their church office telephone on Sunday mornings giving information such as worship service times, times for Sunday school, availability of childcare, etc.).

Advertising can indeed create significant awareness that may attract newcomers to the church. To be effective, it needs to be done regularly and consistently over many years as an ongoing process with the best times being just before Christmas, before Easter, and back-to-school time in the fall. It is essential that the advertising be authentic, genuine, and true. Only then will we create the awareness through advertising that genuinely attracts and connects newcomers to Jesus Christ through the church.

SERVICE EVANGELISM

Service evangelism creates awareness of the church as a caring, serving organization directly meeting the immediate needs of potential newcomers through acts of kindness and service. This style of creating awareness has tremendous potential for most every church, because service evangelism does not require special skills or even the spiritual gift of evangelism (sharing the Christian faith in a winsome way with someone we do not know) in order to participate. You simply need to be willing to help someone else in a tangible, concrete way. For younger generations, the mode for developing awareness is especially appealing for a couple of specific reasons. First, it is short term. The participant in service evangelism can come once on a Saturday morning to help out in a project and does not need to commit to long-term involvement. Second, the participant in service evangelism sees immediately, up close and personal, how she or he makes a difference in someone else's life, which gives particular meaning to the act of service.

Churches are using a wide range of service projects to reach out to others and thereby create a significant and highly attractive sense of awareness within the larger community. One church distributed thousands of bottles of water to persons in the crowd watching the community parade during a hot, summer day. Each bottle had a card attached simply stating that "God loves you and so do we at First United Methodist Church," with Web site, address, and phone number listed. Another church went throughout the neighborhood on a Saturday morning and distributed light bulbs of the recipient's choice, again offering a card with a simple message about "God's light for our lives" and information for contacting the church. A different church held a free car wash on the Saturday before Mother's Day. Each recipient of the free car wash was also given a church contact card, and a few persons were so touched by this simple act of kindness that they came to worship the next morning. Another church has for years offered free gift-wrapping at the local mall for those who purchase gifts there. A sign above the wrapping area identifies the church, which has attracted a growing number of newcomers over the last twenty years.

These are just a few of the growing number of examples of creative service projects undertaken by churches to help increase the community's awareness of the church and its potential for being a place newcomers would consider visiting.

PERSONAL INVITATION

Of all the means that churches may use to increase awareness of their church within the community and to attract newcomers to participate, by far the most effective means is personal invitation. Between 70 to 90 percent of all persons who come new to church to worship do so because of the direct or indirect influence or contact of someone in the life of that church. *The Unchurched American* from George Gallup shares that over half of all persons who are unchurched (have not been in a worship service for at least six months) said that they could see themselves coming to worship at some time in the future if they were invited.[3]

Part of the difficulty with personal invitation as a style of outreach is that we often confuse informing with inviting. Sharing information about the church and its programs and ministries is important, but such sharing of information is not inviting. As one layperson in a local church recently expressed it: "Telling someone to come by for dinner sometime is not an invitation; asking him to come join us at our house for dinner this Saturday night is an invitation!" Invitations are personal, specific, and relational. The genuine invitation is face-to-face or phone-to-phone; it is to a specific event or experience; and it is asking the other person to share that event or experience with us.

The gospel is always a relational gospel; it is about a relation-ship of love that God seeks to have with every person. Personal invitation is a way of expressing that relational love tangibly and concretely. The apostle Paul shared with the church at Thessalonica that "we are determined to share with you not only the gospel of God but also our own selves" (1 Thess. 2:8). So per-sonal invitation is a style of evangelism and outreach consistent with the gospel we share by also sharing ourselves.

Not everyone responds positively to our personal invitation, especially the first time. Just as with advertising, this readiness factor affects personal invitation. What makes persons ready to accept our invitation (or to act on our advertising) are the pre-cipitating life transition events that have occurred recently in their lives. In fact, studies have found that 97 percent of all per-sons coming new to a church have had one or more of these life transition events, typically, within the last month or two.[4] These life transition events are common and happen to us or our fami-lies regularly, including birth, death, marriage, divorce, illness, change of job, change of residence, promotion, loss of job, retire-ment, and other major transitions. These life transition events also produce stress, which motivates us to be willing to change behavior—in this case, to act on the advertising or to accept the invitation. So the life transition events are a precipitant or cata-lyst to readiness for the prospective newcomer. The Readiness Box below illustrates the key role that readiness plays in the effectiveness of a personal invitation.

	We Are Ready	We Are Not Ready
They Are Ready	RESULTS	missed opportunity
They Are Not Ready	wait	no results

For example, if we're ready but they're not ready, then our ministry is to wait—but creatively as we stay prepared for their coming. If we aren't ready but they are ready, then the result is a missed opportunity because the invitation was not issued when it would have been accepted. If we aren't ready and they aren't ready, then nothing will happen and no one will realize what has been missed. But if we're ready and they're ready, then ministry can occur and connection can happen with God's love through the church and its ministry.

There are some specific strategies that churches have based around personal invitation as an effective means of awareness that attracts newcomers. One such strategy is "Bring a Friend Sunday." Several factors help with the success of this strategy. One is to widely promote this event well in advance so persons can consider what friend or friends they will invite to worship on that special Sunday. Another factor is enlisting leadership of the church first to commit to invite friends, family, and neighbors to worship on that Sunday—and having them share with the congregation their willingness and eagerness to invite others to come to worship. It is important to remember that your leaders lead primarily by example.

Joe Harding used a strategy of personal invitation that was highly effective in the United Methodist Church he served as senior pastor in Kirkland, Washington. Twice a year, a few weeks before Christmas and Easter, Dr. Harding would distribute three-by-five-inch index cards to the worshiping congregation that Sunday. He would encourage worshipers during a time of prayer to write down on their index cards the names of up to five persons that they would like to see come to worship with them that Christmas or Easter. He then suggested that those cards be taken home and put in a prominent place where they would be seen at least daily—refrigerator, shaving mirror, makeup mirror, or car dashboard. He urged daily prayer for each person listed on the index cards and for the opportunity and the courage to extend to them a personal invitation to worship. Because of this regular, consistent practice, the church would have an additional worship attendance of 50 percent beyond the normal expectation and experience for those holiday Sundays. Personal invitations can and do make an incredible difference in our ability to create awareness and to attract persons through our relationships to come to church and experience relationship with God.

SUMMARY

Stretching out and reaching beyond our comfort zone toward newcomers in a variety of ways is the crucial beginning of our relay race of assimilation. Without intentional, consistent, varied ways of reaching out into the community and creating awareness that attracts people to come and experience the love of Jesus Christ through the various ministries and experiences of the church—well, the race could be over before we even begin! But we don't need to let that happen. We have a variety of exciting, proven strategies available to us in order to reach out to others in love. So let's get ready, start stretching, keep reaching, and get going.

* * *

Jill Sampson entered the 11:00 AM worship service at First Church just after newcomers Bill and Cathy Johnson and Jennifer Rodriguez. As the staff person of First Church who worked not only with small groups but also with newcomer assimilation, Jill was always running a bit late for worship, since she seemed to find so many last-minute details and conversations that kept her busy on Sunday mornings. That particular Sunday had included an energetic conversation with Steve Collier, a member of her Newcomers Team. Of course every conversation with Steve was "energetic" because he was an enthusiastic new participant on her team. His marketing and computer skills, as well as his Generation X viewpoint, had already added so much to the Newcomers Team. In fact it had been Steve who convinced the Newcomers Team to propose a budget increase for improved newspaper ads, better signage around the building, a new computer program for tracking newcomer assimilation, and the new answering machine in the office with its friendly and helpful message for newcomers who called on Sunday morning. Steve had also introduced the Newcomers

Team to concepts like the "stages of readiness," and he had urged them to be patient with their new awareness efforts. "These things take time," Steve had said, "and we must be persistent and consistent in our efforts to attract newcomers." Jill smiled as she remembered that conversation. "Steve always has a knack for saying things in memorable ways, like 'persistent and consistent.' I guess that's why his own marketing firm is doing so well."

Jill's conversation that morning with Steve had taken a new turn. At last week's meeting of the Newcomers Team, Jill had shared a devotional reading from a book recommended to her by Pastor Jones— Henri Nouwen's Reaching Out—and she had commented in particular about the biblical understanding of "hospitality." Well, Steve had gotten excited about that idea, had purchased the book (online of course) and had already read it twice and wanted to talk with Jill about it. "Such enthusiasm," Jill murmured almost out loud. "I am certainly grateful to have him on my Newcomers Team." She looked forward to the Monday morning meeting of the Newcomers Team, because she was certain that Steve would have other ideas about how to make First Church even more effective in attracting newcomers and welcoming them too.

CHAPTER TWO

Welcoming Newcomers

B ill and Cathy Johnson had already discovered that First Church was a warm and friendly congregation. This fact surprised them, since they had come from a friendly midsize congregation, and never expected to find a similar experience in a larger church. "This is amazing," thought Cathy, "the worship service hasn't even started and already we have been greeted warmly by half a dozen people. I hope that they don't have a time in the service where they put us on the spot as newcomers, because that would certainly spoil the mood of what we have already experienced."

Bill was also thinking about their warm reception, and as usual he was trying to analyze what had happened. He remembered being welcomed by ushers at the entryway doors and that was typical and expected, but in this case, the greeters were unusually polite, friendly, and well informed (they had even quickly described the route to the sanctuary and to the rest rooms), and they had nice large nametags. They were also welcomed by persons who seemed to be "roaming greeters." They also had large nametags with large printing that said "May I help?" Bill liked that touch, and he was impressed that those greeters asked his name, shared a visitor packet, and invited them to stay for the coffee time after worship. Most impressive of all, thought Bill, had been the ushers they encountered as they entered for worship.

Bill had often been an usher himself at Middleton Church, while Cathy was up singing in the choir, so he considered himself something of an "expert" on how to usher. "Those ushers are good," he thought, "and they must have gone through some kind of training. Each of them smiles, asks people where they want to sit, and even offers a friendly handshake." Bill continued to be impressed as he remembered how many different people had already greeted him before the service even started, and he continued to analyze and to compare those efforts.

Cathy was not as analytical about their experience. Instead she was taking in the beauty of the sanctuary. It really was rivaled by the open, spacious entryway with its lovely atrium that had obviously been constructed to join the old sanctuary with the education wing. She had enjoyed the ferns and flowers placed tastefully in that space, and now she also enjoyed the brightly colored banners, the calm but not depressing music that was helping to set the tone for worship, and she even experienced the comfort of the seat and the total surroundings. She was much more introverted than her husband, Bill, but she had also found that various greeters and ushers were friendly and inviting. "They weren't too pushy," she thought, "and yet they did their jobs in a warm way." In fact, "warm" was both the word and the feeling that best described for Cathy her experience thus far at First Church.

* * *

As the worship service began with a lively musical call to worship and the pastor inviting the people to enter into the presence of God, Jennifer Rodriguez found herself surprised that she could follow the service. She had not been inside a church for several years, and she remembered the services in her home church as "boring" and "hard to follow." She remembered as a child how she never was quite sure when to stand, sit, or kneel, and how difficult it had been to make sense out of the worship service. The worship bulletin here at First Church, by contrast, was easy to read, with instructions and notes written in simple, nonchurch language, so Jennifer felt herself relaxing.

She had also found a warm welcome from the greeters and ushers as she arrived after the service had already begun. In fact, it surprised her to find such helpful people were still on duty and quite patient with her and her children. They kindly offered to guide Jennifer to the nursery if she wanted to leave Sammy there, but they had also assured her that "this is a child-friendly place and your children are welcome to remain with you for the worship service." Her two kids wanted to stay with her and seemed already to be feeling at home here. She chose to sit near the back of the sanctuary (and the ushers were polite and helpful in allowing her to do that) where they were near some other young families with children. In fact, Jennifer's children soon discovered that First Church has a children's area in the rear corner of the sanctuary that was filled with "quiet toys" and Bible story sheets that the children could use during worship. Already she sensed that First Church was indeed, as the greeter said, a child-friendly place.

Now as Jennifer continued to relax and to follow the worship service, she was amazed that Pastor Jones's sermon today was part of a series entitled, "Overcoming Life's Challenges." Jennifer could not remember ever hearing a sermon that related so directly to real life, and today's sermon even dealt with divorce. "Oh no," she had thought, "this sermon is going to make me feel even more guilty for my marriage failure." Again she was surprised, as she heard Pastor Jones speak to the issue of divorce with compassion, tenderness, and hope. The sermon lasted nearly twenty minutes, but to Jennifer the time seemed to go quickly because she was so enthralled with the sense of hope and insight she experienced. Almost before she realized it, her tearful eyes had dried and she felt herself smiling for the first time in a long time.

* * *

The fellowship time after worship was in full swing, and the Johnsons were starting to have some doubts about First Church. They noted all of the small groups of people standing around talking with one another, and they were feeling very alone in the midst of that. Bill was realizing how many times back at Middleton Church he had talked with people he knew well and he wondered, "Did I miss opportunities to greet newcomers, just like these folks are doing?" Fortunately, before too much time passed, they were approached by a friendly couple wearing large nametags with the words "Coffee Host" and their own names. This couple turned out to be Clyde and Norma Truman, a retired couple who were not only longtime members of First Church but also active members of the Newcomers Team led by Jill Sampson. Clyde and Norma quickly took Bill and Cathy under their wings, showed them the way to the coffee table (which also had an assortment of sweets and health foods), and also introduced them to several other members of First Church. In fact, Cathy felt so comfortable talking with Norma that they even discussed Cathy's interest in music and her involvement in choir back at Middleton Church. Meanwhile, Bill was sharing with Clyde about his job change, his plan to retire in about twelve years, and his hopes of finding a new church home. Clyde was a good listener who asked helpful questions that were open and not pushy, and then Clyde finally shared his own retirement story and how he had become actively involved in SCORE—a group of business executives who volunteer to help new start-up businesses, especially minority-owned businesses, here in the city. Bill was fascinated to hear about that group, so Clyde offered to send him some material.

On their way home from their first Sunday at First Church, Bill and Cathy discussed their experiences that morning. "I think that I would like to go back there another Sunday to see if our first experience was a good indication of what to expect at that church. How about you?" Bill asked. Cathy agreed, but added some words of caution. "Let's be careful and not make any decisions too quickly. I enjoyed the sermon by Pastor Jones, but I want to hear sermons on some other topics. Divorce is not really our issue—at least not unless you take another job transfer in the next few months!" She was smiling, but Bill understood the message loud and clear. This job change and move to a new community had been tough on Cathy, especially with her recent health issues. Of course they had not mentioned anything as personal as that with those friendly greeters, ushers, and coffee hosts at First Church.

* * *

Jennifer's experience after worship was brief. She was eager to get home and work on her homework for class—she hated to start the week feeling behind on her schoolwork when she also had to work at the café on Monday evening. She was surprised to notice that her two children were not overly eager to leave First Church. One of the other young mothers in the rear seats of the sanctuary was kneeling and talking with them and some other children. She then stood and introduced herself to Jennifer. "Hi, my name is Susie Bloomer, and I was just asking your children if they would like to come to Sunday school next week. It meets at 9:30, and we have a fantastic program. I think that your kids would enjoy it. Could I have someone from the children's ministry call you this week?" *Jennifer was cautious, but Susie's smile was so genuine and inviting that she found herself giving her phone number to Susie with a warning that "I go to school and work afternoons, so I am hard to reach." After Susie replied, "No problem. I know how it is to be busy with kids," their conversation continued and Jennifer enjoyed talking with another mother.*

Jennifer felt relieved as she and the kids left First Church. She had gone reluctantly, afraid that she would not understand church or that she would feel out of place. Instead, she had felt really welcomed. There were not too many places in her life where she felt so affirmed. She could not wait to tell the Larsens at the café tomorrow about her experience at First Church.

* * *

WARMING UP TO NEWCOMERS

After an appropriate time of stretching, the relay team transitions into warming up. Runners get up from the ground and start moving. They begin to break into an easy jog. As the speed increases, they shift into a brief period of sprinting. Then the runners ease up, return to a comfortable jog, and walk. This process is repeated several times to make sure that the muscles are fluid enough to run without strain or injury. Many races have been lost due not to lack of speed but due to lack of adequate warm-up.

The same is true in the life of the church when it comes to assimilating newcomers. We need to make sure that we have "warmed up" in preparation for the arrival of newcomers. It will be important that we are thoughtful, compassionate, and intentional in welcoming the first-time visitors who arrive at our church. The compassion we feel for newcomers needs to be translated into concrete actions of hospitality and welcome. Reaching out through word of mouth, advertising, service evangelism, and invitation is a great start in assimilating newcomers. The next step after this great start is to offer a warm welcome that demonstrates the love of God through our actions of genuine hospitality.

CREATING A CLIMATE OF HOSPITALITY

We are reminded by the Readiness Box in chapter 1 that if we do well in reaching out and they're ready to come, then we must be ready to receive them graciously and treat them with the care and respect due to guests. Our goal is to create a churchwide climate of hospitality that embraces all newcomers who pass through our doors. Creating this climate of hospitality requires intentional reflection and strategy.

We are indebted to Henri Nouwen for his sensitive and powerful insights into the theology of hospitality contained in his book *Reaching Out.*[1] Nouwen begins by reminding us that hospitality creates a free and friendly space for persons to encounter one another. Hospitality is a free space because you are free to be who you are, just as I am free to be who I am. It is a friendly space because we can relate to one another as friends. So hospitality creates an environment where friendship is not only possible but also encouraged and promoted. We accept newcomers as they are, regardless of dress, appearance, background, or social sense. And we are eager to connect with them as friends in Jesus Christ.

In this dynamic climate of hospitality, a marvelous transition takes place. The stranger becomes a guest. This change in our perception of the newcomer lies at the core of hospitality. Too often newcomers are perceived as strangers—someone unknown and therefore suspicious; someone to be treated with caution and kept at a safe distance; someone whom we treat with cautious politeness and keep at a safe emotional distance from the rest of the church family whom we know and trust and love. Hospitality means perceiving the newcomer as a guest—someone to be welcomed and respected, someone to be treated with openness and warmth as a potential friend. Churches that practice hospitality see visitors as guests, welcoming them with open arms and open hearts into the house of God.

Guests are helped to feel at home, just like Abram welcomed the three travelers into his home.[2] Abram saw them through the eyes of hospitality as welcome guests for whom he made room in his home. In the same way, hospitality calls us to make newcomers feel right at home in our church, especially on their first visit. Reflect for a moment on this scenario: Two persons approach at the same time while you are serving as a greeter at your church. One is a longtime, close personal friend from your Sunday school class, and the other is a first-time visitor. Which one are you most likely to greet first and most warmly? Will the answer be different if you practice hospitality intentionally and consistently?

In an environment of hospitality, gifts are given to the guest. Hospitality always offers our best as an expression of genuine welcome. In Genesis 18 we read that Abram and Sarai provided a feast to the three travelers they had welcomed into their home— not leftovers or a quick handshake that sent them on their way still hungry. Hospitality demands that we offer our best gifts to our guests. Do our gifts to our first-time guests in our church include our best welcome or just a perfunctory handshake? Do we offer open conversation or the curt greetings given to someone boarding an airplane? Do we share the best seats in our churches or the leftover ones in the back row in the balcony where you cannot see the preacher? Hospitality urges us to offer our best gifts to our treasured guests. When we do that, our guests are free to offer their best gifts as well. Genesis tells us that the three travelers reciprocated with the great gift of the announcement of a child to be born to Abram and Sarai. Perhaps the newcomers who visit our church and experience our best gifts will also be freed to offer their gifts and talents to the ministry and service of God through the church. Hospitality creates such an environment for both host and guest.

Such a hospitable environment requires what Nouwen calls a "poverty of heart and mind." In order to receive gifts, it is necessary for us to recognize that we do not know it all ("poverty of mind") and we have not experienced it all ("poverty of heart"). Thus, hospitality enables us to see our guests as angels, messengers of God. Hebrews 13:2 states it explicitly: "Do not neglect to show hospitality to strangers, for by doing that some have entertained angels without knowing it." Newcomers to our churches can indeed be angels bearing God's message, but only if we have the eyes and ears and hearts of hospitality that allow us to receive their gifts.

In this hospitable environment, we practice acceptance of newcomers not hostility toward them. Hostility is just mean-spirited or nasty actions. Often hostility within churches is far more subtle and difficult to recognize and correct, based on the presumption that "I will accept you only when you become what I want you to be." By this definition, too much evangelism is hostile, not hospitable, welcoming, or accepting. By contrast, hospitality is rooted in an attitude that says "I will accept you as you are." Hospitable evangelism accepts, welcomes, and befriends people—and leaves to God the role of transforming and changing people. Such acceptance is rooted in compassion. Compassion recognizes that we are much more alike than we are different. This compassion includes not only accepting one another but also confronting one another in honesty. Only then can we discover each other's gifts and grow as friends.

The ultimate reason this is our goal is that hospitality is the way God treats us all. For God indeed is truly the Lord of hosts—the Lord of all of us who are called to be God's hosts for all the guests that God sends our way! So let's look more closely and specifically at how we might create and enhance the climate of hospitality, especially for our first-time visitors.

HOSPITALITY AS NEWCOMERS ARRIVE

For many persons, going to a new church for worship the first time is not easy. For some, it is overwhelming and scary. First-time visitors are not sure how they will be received or treated. They are often concerned that they might be either ignored or pressured. That's why it is so important for the church to be intentionally hospitable from the very moment that newcomers arrive. Hospitable churches effectively assimilate newcomers by understanding and practicing the adage that "worship is not prelude-to-postlude; worship is door-to-door."[3]

A warm welcome starts with the parking lot. Hospitable churches provide ample parking for newcomers, especially first-time visitors. They understand that they need one parking spot for every 1.7 worshipers in the pews.[4] Even if parking space is at a premium, they will use signs to designate parking spots near the church entrance to be reserved for first-time visitors (along with spots reserved for handicapped parking, of course). A few churches even have parking lot attendants (some call them "parking lot ushers") to help people find a parking space. And when it rains, those attendants are armed with umbrellas and are ready to escort worshipers into the church. One church even borrows golf carts on Sunday mornings and uses them to transport people from the far ends of their parking lot up to the door.

The hospitable church also provides visible, attractive signs that easily guide the newcomer to his or her destination—whether that be the sanctuary, the church office, or the nursery. One person shared with us this account of being a first-time visitor to church while on vacation:

> I chose to go to an early service at a nearby church, knowing that would free the rest of the day to relax on the beach. I arrived just before the service was to start, and found no sign to direct me to the sanctuary. I tried seven doors before discovering one that was unlocked! When I finally found the right door to enter, I encountered an usher who barely looked up, just thrust a bulletin into my hands, and left me to find my own way into the sanctuary.

You can believe that most newcomers to your church will not be so persistent to get to worship! Clear signs may make the difference on whether they come and whether they stay.

The building itself can demonstrate that we are ready to welcome newcomers. Is the grass cut? Are the bushes trimmed? Is the snow shoveled? Are the walks cleared? Is the exterior cared for? Are the grounds kept? Now you might ask yourself, "What difference does all of this make?" And the answer from Tom Peters is "the coffee stain syndrome."[5] The coffee stain syndrome occurs when you get on an airplane, perhaps already feeling a bit nervous, and as you sit in your seat you discover a large, dried coffee stain. Assuring yourself that it is indeed dried, you sit down only to find that the foldaway tray won't fold down! And then comes a dreaded, queasy, anxious feeling deep in the pit of your stomach because you're thinking, "If they don't take care of the things I can see, how are they caring for the things that I can't see—like the engine!" Newcomers to your church may wonder, "If they don't take care of things that I can see (like painting, mowing, and shoveling), do they take care of things that I can't see (like Sunday school classes, children's programs, and decision making)?"

Once inside the building, newcomers should be greeted in a narthex that is bright, appealing, and uncluttered. There may need to be "newcomer greeters" or "hosts" whose sole function is to spot, identify, and welcome newcomers to the church. They smile, offer a friendly handshake, introduce themselves, and ask the names of the newcomers to find out if the newcomers have friends or family in the church. They see if the newcomers have any questions that they can answer and offer relevant information, such as the location of the sanctuary, nursery, fellowship hall (for coffee hour), and rest rooms. They escort the newcomers to the sanctuary and introduce them to an usher. All this communicates to the newcomer that we are glad that they decided to come join us for worship.

It is very helpful if the entrance or narthex itself is welcoming, perhaps with a few visuals to express the theme of that day's worship or a significant, upcoming event. One hopes the entrance provides a place for conversation so that several persons besides the greeters will welcome newcomers. All persons in the church have a role in welcoming newcomers, yet some hesitate to approach newcomers because they're not sure what to say. A good option is to say, "Hi, I'm Doug. I don't believe we've met before. How long have you been a member of this church?" This greeting assures newcomers that they look like they fit in and belong here, which is affirming. This is certainly better than saying, "Hi, I'm Doug. I don't believe we've met before. Is this your first Sunday?"—only to insult longtime members by insinuating they look out place and don't belong. Good welcoming space in the narthex can indeed facilitate this conversation, and all members of the church can be encouraged to greet those who are new to them.

Vitally important for hospitality is a hospitable nursery that is clean, comfortable, bright, and secure. Most parents have high standards, especially when it comes to their infants and toddlers. They notice if linens are fresh and clean and if the toys are safe and in good repair. They expect competent, caring, adult supervision in the nursery. For security purposes, they expect a careful system of releasing their children from the nursery only into their care (which means registration, check-in, and checkout). It is crucial that all churches—especially large churches and those in urban settings—have not only security but also safe nurseries in order to be truly hospitable. This must include preventing any problems by carefully screening all who work with children. An example of putting these ideas into practice concerns two parents who took their baby to the church nursery during their first visit. The attendant made them fill out a registration card, placed an identification tag on the infant, and handed the mother the matching tag. The attendant then told the parents to please hold on to the tag because that was the only way they could claim their child from the nursery. Those parents were so impressed with this secure care of their baby that they not only returned the next Sunday but they also told several of their friends about their experience. If your church hopes to reach families with young children, then a hospitable nursery is essential.

Once the newcomers are ready to enter the sanctuary for worship, the ushers become an important part of the hospitality team. Their role is much more than distributing bulletins and taking up the offering. The ushers also greet the newcomers with a smile and handshake and make them feel welcome. They respect newcomers by asking them if they would like to be seated and if so, where they would like to be seated. It is helpful to ask if the newcomers have family, friends, neighbors, or coworkers whom they would prefer to be seated with. To create a free and friendly space in this instance means giving newcomers the freedom to choose where they will sit and with whom. Hospitable ushers treat newcomers as welcome and respected guests.

Such hospitality before the worship service even begins requires a team effort. It includes the groundskeepers, the trustees who maintain the facility, the parking lot attendants, the newcomer greeters, the nursery attendants, the ushers, the narthex display artists, and all persons aware of and sensitive to greeting newcomers wherever encountered on Sunday morning. Hospitable churches understand that it takes a whole team to make hospitality real for newcomers even before the worship service begins. Remember, for the newcomer the experience of worship is not simply prelude-to-postlude, it is door-to-door!

HOSPITALITY DURING THE WORSHIP SERVICE

It is important that the central experience of worship also be one of hospitality, and this has significant implications for the greeting time, the use of language, preaching, ritual, the bulletin, and involvement of children.

A hospitable greeting time requires a careful balance. We don't want to overlook newcomers' presence with us by ignoring them, but we also don't want to embarrass them by putting them on display, especially forcing them to stand and introduce themselves. This is especially true in larger churches because there is more expectation of anonymity. A smaller church is more like a family and newcomers understand it is hard not to be noticed, recognized, and introduced. One approach that seems to deal well with the greeting time in larger churches is to offer a brief time of common greeting for all those gathered, along with some optional opportunity for members and constituents to introduce to the congregation any newcomers they have brought with them.

For the worship service to be welcoming, we need to pay attention to what language we speak. It is helpful to understand and apply the study of neurolinguistics to worship. Although each one of us gathers data about the world in all three modes, we each have a primary mode for communication, based on neurolinguistics: aural (what we hear), visual (what we see), and kinesthetic (what we feel). In the general population, 35 percent of people are primarily aurally oriented, 15 percent are visual, and 50 percent are kinesthetic. In order to connect and communicate effectively with the broad range of newcomers who may visit us on any given Sunday, we must learn to speak their language.[6]

For aural folks, a good sound system is essential, and music will communicate well with them, especially if it is the style they are accustomed to listening to everyday. For visual folks, use of color and good lighting is welcoming; striking banners and colored glass are inviting; and bulletin covers that depict the theme of the morning communicate well to them. For kinesthetic folks, a handshake and a warm greeting are essential for feeling welcome. The greeting time, the passing of the peace, and comfortable seats make them feel right at home. Hospitable churches learn to speak the language of each newcomer, whether aural, visual, or kinesthetic.

It is also important for the language to be understandable. We need to avoid using lots of stilted, "churchy" words so that we can make comprehending and experiencing God in the worship service easier and more understandable for those newcomers who are unfamiliar with theological language. For example, a hospitable pastoral prayer that allows for free and friendly space will be conversational in style and tone, using easily understandable language as the pray-er simply talks with God.

Sermons must also be hospitable by minimizing the use of words that unchurched newcomers would have difficulty understanding. Instead, the preacher can use common words and images (just as Jesus did with his parables) to communicate the message of God in a way that includes rather than excludes. The sermon is a time of talking with the congregation about an issue or topic relevant to their lives from the vantage point of God's word. This creates a free and friendly space for the listener to encounter God amid the message. If the message is hospitable, not hostile, it creates a space for God to work.

Even the bulletin needs to be examined from the perspective of hospitality. The primary function of the worship bulletin or folder is to guide the worshiper through the worship experience. Therefore it is essential for language to be clear and understandable, especially for those with little or no church background. One must never assume the reader already knows the language. A common assumption is listing the Lord's Prayer without including the words, thus assuming everyone already knows the Lord's Prayer and which version we use ("debts," "trespasses," or "sins"). Other examples include listing the doxology without the words (because everyone knows it, of course), the *Gloria Patri* without the words or explanation (who's she, anyway?), and the Scripture reading without the words or page reference (because everyone can find it themselves). Reducing such assumptions will make the worship bulletin much more hospitable. The key here is to design the bulletin with the unchurched newcomers in mind to guide them through the worship service, rather than developing the bulletin just for regularly attending church members.

Another key issue is making assumptions with the announcements. Listing a meeting of UMW means little to a newcomer, especially someone who may not be a member of the United Mine Workers! Another common assumption is presuming everyone knows what a group or committee does and who is involved in it. So even listing "The United Methodist Women will meet at Stella's home on Wednesday night" is not helpful. It is helpful and inviting if we describe the meeting as "a gathering of all interested women for fellowship and study at 314 South Elm Street," along with a time, contact person, and phone number for further details. This kind of announcement says to newcomers that they are welcome to come and participate.

All churches have rituals that help strengthen the bonds of the participants with God and between themselves. Rituals have wonderful power to help people feel a strong sense of belonging. But for rituals to be hospitable for newcomers, it is essential that the rituals be open. Let's further describe what we mean by "open" ritual with a story about communion. A newcomer attended a church for worship because it was of the same denomination she had grown up in. Communion was being served that morning, and as the tray was passed, the newcomer took a cup and drank it. She was stunned to discover that it contained wine rather than the grape juice that she was accustomed to. Not wishing to cause a scene, she simply left and did not return—even though she had been very pleased about everything else with the church. Months later she discovered through a friend that the church that served the wine was a merged congregation. One of the compromises from the merger was to serve both wine and grape juice for every communion. The wine would be in the cups in the outer two rings of the tray and the remaining cups would be filled with grape juice. Unfortunately that particular Sunday morning, the bulletin was particularly full so the description of the choice of cups for communion was deleted, thereby making the ritual "closed" rather than open, inviting, and welcoming. Hospitable churches make their rituals open and inviting by describing both the meaning and process of the ritual.

Hospitable worship is worship that welcomes newcomers to participate fully in the worship experience. Doing so will mean careful attention to the way we greet, the language we use, the openness of our rituals, and the bulletins we use. Such care can make all the difference in whether a newcomer truly feels at home in God's house of worship.

HOSPITALITY AFTER THE WORSHIP SERVICE

Hospitality after the service is also critical if newcomers are to perceive that our hospitality is genuine and not simply a ploy to get them to return. Remember, worship is not just prelude-to-postlude; worship is door-to-door, and the newcomer is not yet back to her car door!

Hospitable churches provide newcomer greeters after the worship service, as well as before. One purpose is to ask for additional information about the newcomer in order to facilitate the followup response (which will be described in a later chapter). Another purpose is to introduce newcomers to other members of the congregation so that we broaden the number of contacts who welcome the newcomer and form potential relationships with him or her within the congregation. Typically, newcomers view a church as very friendly when they have been welcomed by at least seven different people on the first Sunday that they attend. Having your newcomer greeters on duty after worship can increase the chance that newcomers will meet at least seven different people.

The fellowship time can either be a wonderful experience of connecting and relating for the newcomers or an awful time of standing alone on the outside and feeling like they don't belong here at the church. Another personal experience will illustrate the importance of being intentional about hospitality in the fellowship time:

> I was coming to consult with the congregation, beginning by attending the worship service. I asked the pastor not to introduce me so I could experience what it was like to be a newcomer to the congregation. Following the worship service, I was not greeted by anyone other than the pastor. I was not invited to come to the fellowship time, but I went anyway to see what would happen. I stood near the entrance to the long fellowship hall by myself, waiting for someone to notice me, speak to me, or invite me in. I waited five minutes and nothing happened. Undaunted (and therefore unlike most newcomers), I walked into the fellowship hall past several persons to the serving line. There, for the first time, someone other than the pastor spoke to me with these words of greeting: "Coffee or punch?" I took the punch and proceeded for the tables, which were arranged in three rows. I walked slowly past each table, nodding and smiling when others did, ready to speak if spoken to, and waiting to be invited to sit. After circling the entire room once, on my second trip through the room someone finally initiated conversation with me. She was friendly and welcoming, asking about me and finding out this was my first Sunday. And after a nice conversation, she went to sit down with her friends and left me standing alone. Five minutes later and still alone, I left the fellowship hall. That evening during the consultation, one of the questions I asked was "What do you do well as a church?" One of the recurring

answers was "We are a friendly church." I affirmed that to be true because I had observed how friendly they were to each other during the fellowship time. In fact, they had been so friendly and focused on each other that they overlooked me, so I described to them my experience that morning. They were genuinely stunned, with one man saying he never saw me. And he didn't, because he was so engaged in his conversation at the table that he wasn't aware I had walked past him twice in the fellowship hall as a newcomer.

Fellowship time doesn't have to be an experience of isolation for newcomers. Fellowship hosts can play an important role in recognizing, welcoming, conversing with, and connecting the newcomers with others. This is also a wonderful time to invite newcomers to come to Sunday school and offer to go with them (rather than simply informing the newcomer about a Sunday school class they can choose to attend). Hospitable churches are intentional about making the fellowship time a free and friendly space for welcoming and developing relationships.

Conclusion: Leaders Shape Hospitality

In *Leadership and the New Science*, Margaret Wheatley describes the importance of field theory for organizations.[7] Leaders create fields around their values that are experienced consistently throughout the life of the organization. Our goal is nothing less than creating a field of hospitality that extends throughout the entire church so that no matter who the newcomer encounters or where the encounter occurs in the church, the experience of the newcomer is deeply and consistently one of genuine, compassionate, Christian hospitality.

To accomplish this goal will mean developing a system of hospitality that, if done consistently over time, can become a field of hospitality that is no longer driven by leadership, but instead is rooted in the very life and core values of the congregation. This requires intentionally developing the persons, processes, and teams to do the specific acts of hospitality that communicate clearly our warm welcome to newcomers. If a church does this with a hospitality that is focused upon God's love for everyone, then it is ready to identify those newcomers in order to continue the relay race of assimilation.

* * *

The Newcomers Team was having its regular Monday morning meeting. After opening devotions led by Jill Sampson, the group began to listen as Steve Collier excitedly talked about what he had learned from reading Henri Nouwen's book, Reaching Out. As the group members discussed the principles of hospitality, they also began to evaluate the ways in which First Church was warm and friendly to visitors. They talked openly about some areas that needed improvement, especially the fellowship time after each worship service. "I am convinced that we need more coffee hosts now that we are having so many more new visitors," said Clyde Truman. "If Norma and I had not found that nice couple—what was their name?—oh yes, the Johnsons, then I am not sure if they would have stayed around very long. They looked kind of lonely standing there while everyone else had their coffee and talked with longtime members."

"Now Clyde," said his wife Norma, "you make it sound so desperate. We just visited with them like anybody would have done. If we had not talked with them, I am sure that somebody else would have."

"That's just the problem!" Steve blurted out. "Remember what we keep saying about inviting newcomers and welcoming them? Everybody's business is nobody's business. That's why we need this Newcomers Team, and that's why we must organize our efforts. If we just assume that 'everyone' will do it, then I am afraid that nobody will do it."

Jill found herself smiling, once again, at Steve's enthusiasm and also at his clever use of words. "Everybody's business is nobody's business," she thought to herself. "I am going to remember that phrase the next time I invite members to serve on this Newcomers Team, or as ushers or greeters or coffee hosts. We must continue to create a climate in this church where hospitality is natural—but also where it is organized."

identifying
Newcomers

As the Newcomers Team continued its Monday morning meeting, its members focused on one of their key agenda items: identifying newcomers in order to be able to respond to them. Jill Sampson directed their attention to the names of visitors and newcomers compiled from the registration pads in the pews, the guest book from the entryway, the list compiled by the greeters in the church's Welcome Center in the fellowship hall, and the lists submitted by Sunday school teachers.

As usual, they faced the issue of newcomers and visitors who had not given enough information for them to be identified clearly. The team did a little detective work, as Steve Collier called it, looking through the city street directories to find more information about those names, and even making phone calls to church members who apparently had been sitting in the same pews with some of the newcomers. Some of those efforts produced results, but some did not. Jill reminded them, "If some people come to our church and really want to stay anonymous, then we have to give them the freedom to do so. That is part of what we have learned about hospitality. If we cannot find enough information about newcomers to identify them, we will just enter their names into our data bank and watch for other opportunities to know them and respond to them." The data bank she referred to was a simple software-tracking program that Steve Collier had helped the team find and use. In his work at his marketing firm he used such software to track their contacts with customers and potential customers, so it had not been difficult for a "techie" like Steve to adapt it for the church's use.

The team accepted Jill's reminder about allowing newcomers to remain anonymous, but clearly they were concerned about getting as much opportunity as possible to identify such newcomers. As Clyde put it rather succinctly, "If we can't identify them, then it is going to be hard to know them!"

Susie Bloomer, another member of the team, had a sudden inspiration. "Last week was my turn to help the offering counters. I just realized that some newcomers may write a check for the offering, and oftentimes those checks will be imprinted with their addresses and even phone numbers. Could we ask the offering counters to let us know if any such new names appear as they count checks?" The rest of the Newcomers Team looked at one another in amazement, and Jill expressed what they all were thinking: "Why haven't we thought of that one before? If a newcomer puts a check in the offering with that kind of information, it certainly would be fair to use that information to identify him or her wouldn't it?" The whole team congratulated Susie for her quick thinking, and Jill smiled once again with appreciation for the energy, passion, and creativity of her Newcomers Team. They always had a good time at their Monday morning meetings, and they also took seriously the task of identifying and responding to newcomers.

The group continued to look at the list. Jill noted the names of Bill and Cathy Johnson, along with that of Jennifer Rodriguez. "What does anyone know about these names?" she asked.

Clyde and Norma shared what they had learned from their conversation with the Johnsons—about Bill's job change, their move to this city, and even a bit about their previous church experience at Middleton. Norma remembered, "Didn't Cathy say something about our choir and how much she enjoyed being in the choir at her previous church?" Clyde nodded his head and added some additional comments about Bill Johnson and his apparent interest in the SCORE program. Together the Newcomers Team was starting to develop a profile of the

Johnsons, their possible needs and interests, and even some ways to connect with them during a follow-up and response.

Next Jill turned to the name of Jennifer Rodriguez, and Susie shared about her conversation with Jennifer and her children. "I sensed that her children are pretty new to church, so we will want to involve them carefully," said Susie. The group finished sharing their initial profile and identification of Jennifer and her children.

Jill led the team to look at four other names for whom they had too little information to identify and profile. Again, she reminded them of the need to be hospitable and patient with newcomers. "This whole effort to identify newcomers takes time, patience, a little detective work, and a commitment to get to know newcomers in order to help them find their place at First Church," she said. The rest of the team nodded in agreement, and they continued to discuss new ways of learning about the newcomers who might come into the life of First Church.

* * *

GETTING OFF TO A GOOD START

The time is imminent for the race to begin, and the runner of the first leg moves to take position at the starting line. All the practice, all the conditioning, all the stretching and warm-up has been in preparation for this moment. The runner places one leg in front and one leg behind, digging in for a strong start. The all-important baton is gripped securely in one hand. The eyes are focused down the track toward the teammate who will next receive the baton. The goal is simple: get your team off to a strong start and, one hopes, even the lead in the race. After taking the mark, the runner rises into the set position at the starter's instruction. With the sound of the starter's pistol, the runners leap down the track toward their teammates.

Your church's newcomer assimilation team also needs to get off to a good start. The assimilation process begins by identifying the newcomers when they arrive at church for the first time. Unless we first identify those newcomers to our church, we cannot respond to them or assimilate them or assist in their faith journey.

A strong start is essential for a good finish, both in a relay race and in assimilating newcomers.

BEYOND RECOGNITION TO IDENTIFICATION

The process of identifying newcomers is really an extension of the ministry of hospitality. Our desire to identify newcomers is a part of the welcome and care we provide for those who are guests in our midst. It is important that we not embarrass newcomers in our attempts to identify who they are. For example, most people are reluctant to stand and be introduced at the beginning of the worship service, so we need other, more hospitable ways to discover the newcomers in our midst. We don't want to use a process of identification that does not make our guests feel at home! Sensitivity in this area is extremely important so that newcomers are not turned off by our efforts to identify them. For those newcomers who wish to remain anonymous, it is essential that we give them the hospitable space to do so. When they're ready for us to identify them, they will let us know.

However, being hospitable in our style of identifying newcomers does not give us permission to be lackadaisical in our efforts. Indeed, we need to be diligent in focusing upon the newcomers among us as an expression of our care and welcome. We need to be ready to respond when they are ready to be identified—and most ready to do so the first time that they attend our church.

It is significant to note that there is a big difference between recognizing newcomers and identifying newcomers. Recognizing newcomers is simply noticing that someone is here who has not been here before. For example, a longtime member might notice someone in the narthex whom she has not seen before. If that longtime member has been versed and trained in the fine art of hospitality, she might even make her way across the narthex to greet the newcomer, express pleasure that the newcomer has chosen to come this morning for worship, and try to make the newcomer feel welcome and at home. Now all of this is helpful and very hospitable, but this is not the same as identifying the newcomer.

The key difference between recognizing newcomers and identifying newcomers is clear, simple, and yet profound: learning their names. Identifying newcomers means discovering and using their names. Without their names, we can still do meaningful hospitality and provide a sense of welcome, but we cannot continue the relay race of assimilation. Discovering the name of the newcomer is the key focus of the identification process. It is the "baton" that we need to discover and then pass on to the next team in the assimilation process. Just as the relay race cannot continue without having the baton to pass along to the next runner, so also our assimilation of newcomers is dependent upon discovering who they are, beginning especially with their names.

THE IMPORTANCE OF A NAME

A person's name plays an important and central role in that person's identity. Hospitality reminds us that the newcomer is to be perceived and welcomed as a guest rather than treated as a stranger. Perhaps the key factor in hospitality is what name we give to newcomers—are they a stranger and potential enemy, or are they a guest and a potential friend? The process of hospitality begins with the amazing transformation that occurs with the name that we give to newcomers.

The Bible continually stresses the centrality of the name to the identity of the person. Jacob means "supplanter" or "cheater." Mary means "corpulent" or "pregnant." Naomi means "pleasant one." And Jesus means "God will save God's people." In a real sense, to know a person's name is to know and identify the person. The name is more than a convenient label that we use; it is the essence of the person.

There is deep within us a longing to belong, and part of that means being known by name. Newcomers who arrive at the church are searching for a connection to God but also a connection to other human beings. If people simply smile and welcome and greet me but never come to know my name, then what is communicated to me is that I do not belong. When instead people extend themselves to get to know me through my name, I experience a genuine invitation to belong. When people also share their names with me, it is a further invitation to relationship and to belong.

NAMES AND NAMETAGS

If names are so important, then what about using nametags for newcomers? It is true the nametags facilitate finding out the names of newcomers, but the drawback is making newcomers feel awkward and on display, causing unintended embarrassment that might even lead to their decision not to return to the church. If nametags are used with newcomers, it is certainly more hospitable to make it clear that wearing the nametag is optional and voluntary. It is even better if a greeter at a welcome center is available to fill out the nametag for the guest (to help avoid illegible handwriting). It is most hospitable to offer nametags to guests only if everyone else is wearing nametags as well (so that the nametag of the newcomer doesn't stand out).

The key to a good system for identifying newcomers is one that helps us obtain the name of the newcomer in a hospitable manner. There is other information that can be extremely important in getting to know the newcomer, including such things as where they live, how long they have lived in the community, names of other family members and ages of children, where they work, and interests and hobbies. But the primary goal of identification is to find out the name of the newcomer. It is the "baton" we need to continue the relay race. Without the name of the newcomer it is very difficult to continue the process of assimilation. Sometimes this requires us to enter into the important spiritual discipline of waiting until the newcomer is ready to be known. But our waiting needs to be active waiting, being prepared in a variety of ways to discover the names of the newcomers who arrive at our church through a variety of different and often overlapping strategies.

DISCOVERING NAMES IS A TEAM EFFORT

Just as a track and field relay race requires several members to make up the team, so also the process of assimilation is a team effort. An effective process of identifying newcomers often includes several strategies to minimize the chance that any newcomer might be overlooked and leave unknown. So let's look at a range of options for identifying newcomers, keeping in mind that you probably won't use them all but will want to select several of these options that best fit the size and style of your congregation.

One option for identifying newcomers that many congregations already use is the formal guest registry book located in the narthex or entryway. Often it is on a stand next to an usher or greeter who encourages the newcomer to sign it. This works relatively well in smaller, family-style congregations, especially in smaller communities. But even then there are a number of newcomers who choose not to sign the guest book and for whom it seems strange and awkward, especially those with little church background (who are the very folks we most want to welcome, identify, include, assimilate, and disciple).

Other churches have also developed a welcome and information center, which is especially useful in larger congregations with an adequate gathering space. Here newcomers are drawn to attractive displays of upcoming events and opportunities, as well as friendly persons ready to assist and answer a variety of questions that newcomers may have. The attendant at the welcome center can ask for the newcomer's name, carefully recording it to be entered into the newcomer database. The welcome center then acts as an extension of hospitality into the area of identification in a way that is not obtrusive but is inviting and responsive.

Roving greeters (in addition to those greeters who simply stand at the door of the church and shake hands) are another way to welcome and identify newcomers. Their sole responsibility is to watch carefully for persons they do not recognize, to make them feel welcome, and to identify who they are by discovering their names. The qualities that make for good roving greeters include having an outgoing personality, being at ease meeting persons they do not know, having enough tenure with the congregation to allow them easily to detect when newcomers are present, and having the gift for conversation that allows newcomers to share themselves in a nonthreatening and unobtrusive way. Our best example of roving greeters was found in a church that had two such persons named Ed and Earl. They knew the congregation, loved to meet and greet new persons, enjoyed getting to know them, and had a great memory for names. If you visited the church once and returned weeks later, Ed or Earl would greet you by name and ask a question related to your previous conversation with them. Now if you don't have an Ed or Earl handy, you can still find extroverted, friendly persons willing to extend themselves to identify newcomers. They can be trained to use a key conversation starter (when approaching someone they do not recognize), saying something like "Good morning. My name is Kim Johnson. I don't think we've had the pleasure of meeting before. How long have you been a member here?" Notice that this statement neither assumes the person is a newcomer ("Are you new here?" or "Is this your first Sunday?"), nor does it imply that he or she stands out as someone who doesn't belong. This kind of statement also avoids risking potential embarrassment (especially in a larger congregation with multiple worship services) in case the person is a longtime member who takes offense at appearing not to be connected to the congregation. Instead, such a conversation starter actually compliments newcomers by assuming they belong here because they look like they fit in and are part of us. It is always better to compliment the newcomers than to irritate the longtime members!

Another method for identifying newcomers is the use of registration pads or pew pads. These pads are passed among the worshipers to register attendance by signing their names (often with space for address, telephone number, E-mail address, prayer requests, and requests for additional information). One advantage of using pew pads is the opportunity to discover significant information about newcomers in a nonthreatening way, as well as the chance for others around them to discover their names when the pad is passed down the row. On the other hand, a disadvantage is this same lack of privacy, and therefore some newcomers will be reticent to sign it. Another disadvantage comes if the members of the congregation fill out the pew pad sporadically, because they will set a negative model and the newcomers likewise will not sign the pads. One way to significantly increase the likelihood that newcomers (and members) will actually sign the pew pad is to set aside a time during the worship service when the pads are intentionally distributed.

Some churches have started using information slips in the bulletin or worship folder rather than pew pads. The information slips are more private, allowing newcomers the opportunity to share information that they might be hesitant to place in a book that is circulated. But that also means that they can more easily avoid putting down any information, including their names, on their slips. Once the information slips are filled out, they are placed in the offering plates, making collecting the information easy and acceptable to newcomers. This system also works best when there is a specified time in the worship service to fill out the information slip, so the newcomer sees everyone else doing this. The congregation's participation with the information slips has a significant impact on whether or not the newcomers fill out their slips. By filling out the slips, everyone can help with newcomer identification.

Section hosts are another way to help identify newcomers. These persons function in a similar way as the roving greeters, and they are particularly helpful if there is a greeting time during the worship service. The section hosts are seated in different areas of the worship space with responsibility for those seated in their section. Like the roving greeters, the section hosts initiate conversation with newcomers, using a similar conversation starter. Section hosts are particularly helpful in larger congregations with a sanctuary where newcomers could be overlooked and left feeling awkward during the greeting time. Again, it is the role of section hosts to try learning the names of newcomers.

After the worship service has concluded, it is important to continue the process of identifying newcomers. This is particularly important because many newcomers arrive just before the worship service begins. Often they do this intentionally to avoid repeating any bad experience that they may have had, such as either being ignored and overlooked or feeling overwhelmed with attention and highly pressured. As a response to this, you may choose to have the roving greeters available and active in the gathering space after the worship service also to welcome and identify newcomers. In addition to this, another possibility is to assign coffee time hosts in the fellowship space during the fellowship time. These persons do in the fellowship space what the roving greeters do in the gathering space: greet people whom they do not recognize, initiate conversation with them, and try to learn the person's name. It is important to be intentional in your hospitality and identification of newcomers during the fellowship time, rather than assume that it will simply happen naturally and automatically.

Another possibility for newcomer identification is the use of over-the-shoulder greeters. This process has proven particularly helpful in larger congregations where the pastor may have enough tenure to distinguish the newcomers from the members and constituents, but where the situation of greeting everyone after worship prevents meaningful conversation at that moment. In such settings, the pastor may have a team of over-the-shoulder greeters standing with the pastor, ready to be quickly assigned to newcomers, to welcome them, engage them in further conversation (remembering to write down their names and other pertinent information), and invite and escort them into the fellowship time if they choose to participate in it. Such a team of over-the-shoulder greeters can provide a transition that allows the pastor to have further conversations later with the newcomers.

Another key group of persons to include intentionally as part of the team to identify newcomers are the Sunday school teachers. Sometimes the first contact that a person or family has with the church is through the Sunday school and not the worship service. So working with Sunday school teachers to gather pertinent information (including, of course, their names and addresses so that the church can send them listings of class announcements and activities, their phone numbers, and parents names in cases where the teacher teaches a children's class) about those who attend their classes for the first time can be a tremendous asset in identifying newcomers. This is also true of small-group leaders because sometimes the first contact with the church is a small group. Especially in larger churches, this is becoming more and more common because people are looking for places to belong and connect; classes and groups provide a great opportunity for this to occur.

Don't overlook the church's financial secretary or the offering counters as potential members of the newcomer identification team. These are the persons who will first see a check that is written by a newcomer and placed in the offering plate. Often that check will not only have the name or names of the newcomers, it will also have other pertinent information helpful to the assimilation process such as an address and telephone number. Such information is "free" information that is available to identify and connect the newcomer.

And finally, all this effort and energy must be focused through the consistent use of a well-developed newcomer database. It makes little difference if we discover the names of newcomers if we cannot remember them and follow up on them. Having such a database where the names of newcomers are consistently entered and the process of their assimilation clearly recorded and tracked is helpful for most every church and absolutely essential in larger congregations. The database should allow a variety of information about the newcomer to be easily entered and accessed to facilitate a consistent and thorough process of assimilating newcomers. The information should include data such as name, address, telephone number, E-mail address, date and place of the first contact, and general notes of relevant, nonconfidential information gained through initial conversation. The database will also be able to track all the helpful additional information about the newcomers and assimilation steps taken by the church, which we will describe throughout the rest of this book. Again, all this information is helpful and important to track, but it is a moot point to have it without also having the person's name. It is the "baton" that is essential to hand off to the waiting Response Team that is ready to run the next leg of our relay race of newcomer assimilation.

POSTSCRIPT TO IDENTIFICATION

A fitting summary of the issue of identifying newcomers can be found in the theme song for the television show *Cheers*. Everyone wants to be "where everybody knows your name." The goal for newcomer identification is to help each newcomer to be known and to belong. The hope is for our churches to be places of hospitality where newcomers can take a break from their troubles and worries, find the strength and encouragement from God, and discover that other people are just the same; to find a place where people know your name and know you and care about you. This is why it is so important for us to identify newcomers.

* * *

As the Newcomers Team prepared to conclude its meeting before lunch, team members looked over the list of names in front of them. Some of these "names" were starting to become real people to them, as they worked week after week with the list. In some cases, a name would appear as a newcomer just one Sunday, not reappear for many weeks, and then suddenly reappear on their list. Such patterns were becoming familiar to the Newcomers Team, and they were getting to be rather skilled at their "detective work" as they called it, trying to learn as much as possible about those names on their list.

Today's meeting concluded with more discussion about the names of Bill and Cathy Johnson and Jennifer Rodriguez. The team was starting to develop a profile of each of those persons; more than just a name, a real sense of identity. It helped Jill and the others to picture those persons, to imagine what their needs and hopes and dreams might be, and then to hold those names—those persons really—in their prayers.

As Jill led them in prayer at the close of this part of their meeting, she invited each team member to ask for God's guidance with these newcomers. "Let us learn to know them as real people, as friends, as companions in the journey of faith. And help us, O God, to respond to these persons in a way that will enhance their spiritual quest. Amen." The whole group added its "Amen" to the prayer, and team members turned to lunch with the rest of the church staff where they would share these new names and begin planning an appropriate response to each one.

Responding to Newcomers

The Monday lunch meeting of the Newcomers Team and the First Church staff was in full swing. As usual, it included lots of laughter, stories from the previous day's services and activities, and plenty of free-flowing information. It had become the pattern for members of the Newcomers Team to conclude their meeting over lunch with the rest of the staff, as a way for them to include the staff in their efforts to respond to the newcomers they had identified. Not only did this allow the Newcomers Team to enroll the help of the staff in learning more about each of the newcomer names on their list, but it also kept the staff involved in the plans for responding to those newcomers. Another unspoken benefit from those Monday lunches was the simple fact that it kept the issue of assimilating new disciples before them as a primary focus of their work and ministry.

It had been Pastor Lindsey Jones who brought to the staff this plan for meeting every Monday around the issue of responding to newcomers. At first there had been some resistance, including a few staff members who were used to taking Mondays off. However, Pastor Jones had come to First Church nearly five years ago, and during that time there had been something of a revitalization of the old downtown church. Many of the lay leaders of the congregation attributed that to the fact that Pastor Jones was a second-career pastor whose business *background, excellent communication skills, and deft work in restructuring the staff had brought about a renewed vitality, a clearer focus upon mission, and a sense of dedication to the whole issue of welcoming newcomers to First Church. In the face of such a movement, and with a few changes in the staff, the current staff members were all on board with the idea of these Monday lunches. Perhaps it also helped that Naomi Bartlett, the office manager and administrator for the staff, always made sure that the lunches were delicious and healthy too. By now, no one on the staff or the Newcomers Team wanted to miss these lunches!*

Another aspect that made the Monday lunch scene so attractive was the enthusiasm and energy of the music director, Kyle Overstreet. Kyle had been on staff nearly five years before Pastor Jones arrived, but the pastoral transition had been a smooth one, and Pastor Jones regarded Kyle as a pastor's dream to work with. When asked by other pastors to define that statement, Pastor Jones would describe Kyle this way: "He is a music director who sees himself in ministry, and his avenue for that ministry just happens to be music. That is such a different attitude from some music directors and organists who see themselves as musicians who happen to be employed by the church." From his perspective, Kyle had been thrilled to find Pastor Jones such a skilled team leader who made wise use of the entire staff. Kyle had also learned a great deal from Pastor Jones about involving people in the ministry of the church through music—so much so that the music program had grown and then doubled during the past five years.

On this Monday, Kyle was in his usual form, describing his experience on Sunday with the Cherub Choir (often jokingly referring to them as the "Shrub Choir"). His obvious love for the children, for music, and for ministry in general was infectious. It was Naomi who brought a more serious note as she reminded everyone, "Newsletter articles are due by Wednesday!" Now that First Church had gone almost entirely to electronic media for newsletters, Web sites, and E-mail communication of important notices, it seemed almost anachronistic to talk about a "newsletter," but everyone knew she was referring to their electronic newsletter that was sent to over 80 percent of their list of members, friends, and constituents. The remaining 20 percent still received their newsletters the old-fashioned way through the U.S. mail.

Jill also reminded the group that they needed to finalize their plans to respond to the three names on this week's newcomer list: Bill and Cathy Johnson and Jennifer Rodriguez. After a lively discussion, they decided that each of the three would receive the typical Monday night phone call (with Susie being on schedule for those calls this week), and then each would also receive an invitation from someone in the church to an activity or group that seemed best to fit their profile of interests or needs.

"Let me call Cathy and invite her to choir," said Naomi. "I understand from your profile that she used to sing in a choir at their previous church, and I am sure she would enjoy being a part of our choir." In addition to serving as a first-rate office administrator, Naomi was also an active member of the sixty-voice Sanctuary Choir at First Church. "OK," said Jill, "but let's wait until Susie makes the phone call tonight, so that we can make sure we have the correct information about her." Jill continued, "How about Bill Johnson? Who would make the best contact with him?" Clyde responded quickly, "I visited with him during coffee time, and he sure seemed interested in the SCORE program in town. Our men's breakfast group is having a speaker from SCORE in two weeks. How about if I invite Bill to that?" The whole group nodded in agreement.

"And now," said Jill, "how about Jennifer Rodriguez? We don't have a lot of information about her, except that she is apparently a single mom with two kids." Susie quickly added, "Two adorable children!" The entire group discussed how best to invite Jennifer to become involved in a group, class, or activity in the church. They finally settled on their new singles group, and they determined that Kyle would be a good contact. In addition to being music director, Kyle was the staff person who provided support for all of the singles programs. "Are we sure that a singles group is really our best bet?" asked Susie. "It seemed to me that she has her hands full with those two kids, no matter how adorable they are. Maybe our mom's group would be a better choice for her. You know that Colleen Damsky is their leader, and she is just about Jennifer's age." The group members discussed the options for a while, and finally settled on the singles group, but they also noted in the database that a secondary option would be the mom's group.

As the luncheon concluded, Pastor Jones offered a few words of appreciation to everyone for their commitment to making First Church the kind of place where newcomers are not only invited and welcomed, but also the kind of place where efforts were made to respond to those newcomers to guide their faith journey. Once again, the group left with a sense of mission and even urgency about making their response contacts to the newcomers.

* * *

THE RACE TO RESPOND

The first runner has almost completed the first leg of the race. The second runner is in position, looking back at his teammate who is fast approaching the exchange zone. The timing for the first handoff is critical. So the second runner looks back and begins striding forward as his teammate extends the baton into his reaching grasp. The second runner's hand closes tightly on the baton just as he hits full stride two steps from the end of the exchange zone. The next leg of the race is off to a great start.

The same is true of the relay race for assimilating new disciples. The handoff after the first leg is critical to continuing the race. In this case, the "baton" is the name of the newcomer obtained in the process of identification. Getting this valuable information about the newcomer in an accurate and timely fashion to the persons who will do the initial response is essential for the next leg of the assimilation process to be successful. Speed is a key ingredient for effective response.

RESPONDING TO THE EMOTIONAL INVESTMENT OF NEWCOMERS

It requires a great deal of emotional investment on the part of the newcomer to take the initiative to come to a church for the first time. Many churches underestimate how difficult it is for a newcomer to take this step. Newcomers have so much uncertainty and anxiety about what they will experience when they arrive. They could be ignored and overlooked, or they could be overwhelmed and pressured, both of which are uncomfortable and a cause for concern. The reality is that the easiest way to avoid these negative experiences is not to go to a new church for worship (which is why invitations, advertising, and service evangelism are so important for newcomers). So it takes significant courage for a newcomer to simply show up and hope that the experience at worship will be positive, affirming, and worthwhile. One woman shared that she actually drove to the church three Sundays in a row, parked her car in the church lot, but simply could not bring herself to get out of the car and go into the building. Instead she drove home twice before finally getting up the nerve to exit her car and go inside the church on her third attempt. Once inside the church she discovered a warm, friendly, inviting place. But she did not know that before she went inside, which was the cause of her reluctance and fear. Her story is not unique. It is not at all unusual for newcomers to be hesitant about attending a church for the first time, and we as the church need to understand this and respond accordingly.

When the newcomer goes home after being at the new church on Sunday morning, he or she is waiting to see how the church will respond to the contact and relationship he or she initiated. If the experience at church on Sunday morning was positive, then the newcomer is thinking: "I like them; I wonder if they like me, too." The church's response is an opportunity to build on a relationship that has been started with the newcomer. The church's response takes that relationship another step, or another "lap" on the race of assimilation. The initial response that we make to those newcomers is about demonstrating our desire for them to continue to be a part of us. It is not about "selling" them on our church and its programs and ministries. For our response to be one of integrity and hospitality, the focus must be on them, not on us.

CHOICES OF RESPONSE

Churches have a variety of choices about the kind of response they will make to the newcomers who have visited them for worship. Unfortunately, one of the most common responses that churches make is to do nothing. The reason most often given for this choice is that the church does not want to appear to be pushy or overly aggressive. Such intent is understandable and admirable. But instead this communicates that the church either does not care about the newcomer or does not want the newcomer to become a part of the church. In such cases the newcomer hears this message and responds by not returning to the church. It is important to realize that newcomers experience pushiness and aggressiveness by the style with which we respond—and not by the speed with which we respond.

Many other churches simply send a letter—often from the pastor—to those who visit them for the first time, expressing appreciation for coming to worship and inviting the newcomer to return to worship again at his or her earliest convenience. This letter is a good form of response, and far superior to doing nothing! Some other churches mail copies of their newsletters to first-time visitors to inform them about upcoming opportunities and possibilities for involvement. This is also a positive response, which can be helpful for some newcomers. But neither of these forms of written communication is the best response that a church can make to first-time visitors. Letters and newsletters are not personal and relational enough to be the kind of welcoming response that will continue to connect newcomers to us as a church.

The best response is a personal, interactive response, which continues to build our relationship with the newcomer as a warm expression of a hospitable love of God in Jesus Christ. This response can be made effectively by either a visit or a telephone call. Which will be most effective for your church depends upon at least three factors: (1) the demographics of the ministry area (urban or rural), (2) the size of the church, and (3) the age of the newcomer. The more urban the area, the larger the church (250 or more in average worship attendance), and the younger the newcomer (45 years old or younger), the more likely that a telephone call will be the more appreciated form of response by newcomers to your church. The more rural the area, the smaller the church (125 or fewer in average worship attendance), and the older the newcomer (55 years old or more), the more likely that a personal visit will be better received by your first-time visitors. You may need to experiment to see if telephone calls or personal visits are more effective in helping newcomers return to worship for a second visit. Remember, the specific goal of the initial response to newcomers is to have them feel welcome so they will return for worship. Any other connections that a newcomer may make as a result of your response are a bonus, but the goal of our response is to let them know we care so they will feel welcome to return.

THE PROCESS FOR RESPONSE

A primary source for responding to newcomers is the book *Fishing on the Asphalt* by Herb Miller. Miller also describes an effective response with the "3 Be's": be brief, be bright, and be gone![1] Be brief: take only five minutes or so to express appreciation for the newcomer's visit to worship, give him or her a gift from the church (perhaps baked goods or a plant), and offer a small pamphlet about upcoming activities and opportunities for involvement at the church. Be bright: be upbeat and positive about the church and your gratitude for their willingness to come and share a Sunday morning with us. Be gone: don't linger after you have done what you came to do. The longer you stay for this visit, the less likely it is that the newcomer will return. Even if the conversation is cordial and engaging, what the newcomer will sense is the scent of desperation on the part of the church visitor (we seem so desperate for new members that we'll come to your house and stay an hour or more at your home after only your first visit in order to convince you to come back and join us). A good response by phone or in person follows these 3 Be's.

Churches often ask what is the best gift to offer to a newcomer in this initial response. Our experience is that the best gift is one that your church feels passionate and excited about giving. It could be a pie or cake, cookies or brownies, a plant or a flower, or perhaps a church pen or a refrigerator magnet (with pertinent church information on it—perhaps even in the shape of the out-line of the church building) that can be sent in the mail along with a brochure after your telephone call. Any of these gifts will work fine if it represents what you wish to share with your new-comers. It is the spirit of the gift that makes it a good gift, a gift that you want to give as an expression of God's love for the new-comer.

Churches often ask about the brochures they give or mail to newcomers. These brochures should not be professionally printed (unless it is a folder with information sheets slipped inside). The reason has nothing to do with quality or expense, but rather the accuracy of the information in the brochure. Having it profes-sionally printed usually means having it printed in large quanti-ties, and by the time a church distributes all of these brochures, some of the information within will be inaccurate, often shortly after it is printed. This is true not only in larger churches, but in smaller ones as well. Instead, we recommend that churches use their own computers and printers to design and print their own brochures in small quantities, so all the information can be kept up to date and accurate and new information can be easily added. Remember, the most important thing about the church brochure you give to newcomers is not its gloss or glitz but its accuracy.

The content of the brochure might include upcoming activi-ties that would be attractive to newcomers, ongoing programs that help newcomers connect with others in the church (like Sunday school classes, Bible studies, choirs, and fellowship groups), or special events (such as music programs, dinners, sea-sonal worship services, and churchwide fellowship events). The brochure could feature the Sunday schedule of activities, includ-ing worship services, Sunday school classes, children and youth activities, and Bible studies or small groups. It is important to share pertinent information, but not too much information, which might overwhelm the newcomer. The language of the brochure should be written so that unchurched persons can eas-ily understand it. Avoid acronyms that mean little to newcomers, and instead give descriptions of the events in a way for newcomers to understand what will occur and decide whether or not to participate. Remember, the brochures are for newcomers and not longtime members, so develop them accordingly.

SPEED OF RESPONSE

In a relay race, speed is a key factor. Speed is also a key factor when it comes to assimilating newcomers. We need to be prepared to respond quickly once we have received the names of the first-time worship visitors. A muffed handoff even at this early stage of the race can make all the difference in how we finish.

Some churches are concerned that moving too quickly can be perceived as being pushy and pressuring the newcomer. So their tendency is to be low-key and wait a week or two before responding. They may even convince themselves that such strategy is theologically sound and pragmatic. But the reality is that such a delay signals a lack of concern and care on the part of the church. The result is just the opposite of our intention: most first-time visitors don't return to the church that they experienced as unresponsive and unconcerned for them.

Herb Miller reminds us of the importance of a speedy response to first-time visitors that is neither overwhelming nor high pressure (the 3 Be's). His experience shows that if a first-time visitor is contacted personally within 36 hours after a hospitable worship experience at the church, there is about an 80 percent chance that she or he will return again for a future visit to worship (sometimes after several weeks while she or he compares the worship experiences with other churches). If personal contact is made between 36 and 72 hours later, there is still about a 60 percent chance that the newcomer will worship again with your church. The percentage of possibility for a newcomer to return continues to decline sharply the longer it takes for the local church to make its response contact. And if your church waits a week or more to make its initial response to the first-time visitor, the chance she or he will return for worship drops to less than 15 percent—the same percentage rate a church gets if it makes no response at all. If you wait a week to make your response you might as well not bother, because the window of opportunity for your response has already closed.

Let's add another factor to this equation of the initial response. Who makes the initial response also makes a difference. In many churches, it is a pastor who makes the initial response by telephone call or personal visit. After all, the pastor is a trained professional in the area of care. The pastor often has the greatest knowledge of the life of the church, including its programs, ministries, and opportunities for involvement, and so could effectively help the newcomer connect with the church. And the pastor is available to take on this responsibility as a part of his or her ministry profile. So at several levels it seems to make sense for the pastor to make the initial response. However, Herb Miller has observed that if the pastor, rather than a trained layperson, makes the initial response, then you can take all the percentages from the paragraph above and cut each of them in half. The reason for this seems to be that the pastor's visit, while appreciated, is expected by the newcomer as part of the pastor's job. Therefore that initial response by the pastor does not seem to have the impact that the same visit by a layperson does, because the layperson is not expected to make the visit as part of her or his job, but rather is doing the visit as an act of voluntary hospitality and care. Laypersons make more effective initial response contacts, and so laypersons need to be trained and equipped to do this ministry.

TRACKING THE PROCESS

Churches that are effective in their ministry with newcomers usually do an excellent job of tracking the process. They do not take for granted that this process will automatically occur without intentional design and consistent and constant monitoring. Once newcomers have been identified, effective churches have an organized system for continuing to connect with newcomers, and they monitor that system regularly. They keep track of who was assigned to make the initial response, when the initial response was made, and any pertinent information gained from that contact that will be helpful in the process of assimilation. Smaller churches may keep this information on index cards; larger churches will undoubtedly track their assimilation processes on computers. Either way, the information needs to be current, accurate, and available to the persons involved in the assimilation ministry. This information is a key "baton" to be handed off many times among the members of the team in order for the team to be successful.

SUMMARY

One of the most poignant moments during the Academy Awards presentation occurred several years ago. Stunned and jubilant, Sally Field made her way to the stage to accept her award. As she approached the microphone beaming with excitement, she shared the sentiment that she has become unintentionally famous for: "I can't deny the fact that you like me! You like me!" Her reaction resonated with most of us and our longing to experience that same sense of: "You like me!" We long for acceptance and affirmation, not just of what we do but especially of who we are. This sense of acceptance and affirmation is also what newcomers are hoping to experience when they come to a church for the first time. And the churches try to express that acceptance and affirmation through our hospitality when newcomers come for worship. We also want to express such acceptance and affirmation through our initial response after they return home. Our initial response is our way of saying to them not only "We like you!" but also to say in a deep and personal way, "God loves you!"

* * *

Susie was always a bit nervous and also excited when she made her Monday night phone calls to the newcomers who had first attended worship on the previous day. She was well aware that her phone call was the start of an important response to each newcomer, and she also

knew that the church's response would be a significant factor in helping each newcomer to feel welcome and ready to return to the church.
Each Monday when it was her turn to make these phone calls, she kept
her schedule free, she prayed to prepare herself, and she actually prac-
ticed aloud her opening statements to each newcomer.

The Newcomers Team had begun making these phone calls with
an actual script that had been developed in consultation with various
business leaders in the congregation. In addition, the Newcomers
Team had held practice sessions where they role-played being a newcomer who was called by a church volunteer. Their practice included
sitting back-to-back, so that they could only hear the voice of the
other person and not see his or her body language, because that practice best simulated an actual phone call. Susie Bloomer had become
quite skilled at these phone calls, perhaps because she took the task so
seriously.

Her phone call with Cathy Johnson went well. As usual, Susie
began by saying, "Hello, is this Cathy Johnson? My name is Susie
Bloomer, and I am one of the volunteers on the Newcomers Team
from First Church. I understand that you were in attendance at our
11:00 AM worship service yesterday, and I am calling to say how much
we appreciate your attendance and to see if there is any other information about our church or community that might be helpful to you."
This opening statement was followed by the most important part of the
phone call: a pause that allowed the newcomer to share whatever he or
she wanted to share. During their training, the Newcomers Team
members had learned how important it was to listen to the newcomer,
rather than to fill up any silence with too much of their own talk or trying to "sell" their church.

During the call with Cathy, Susie learned that Bill and Cathy had
moved to the city from Middleton, where they had been involved in
their previous church. Susie also sensed that Cathy was having some
struggles adapting to the move, and Cathy voiced her hope that finding a "church home" would help them to feel at home in their new
residence. Susie carefully asked, "What kinds of things were you
involved in at your previous church?" and she learned that Cathy had
indeed been very involved in the choir there. She also learned that
Cathy's husband, Bill, was not interested in choir, but rather had

been involved in things like Trustees, a men's group, and other service projects. Susie took careful notes, in order to add to the profile
that was being developed by the Newcomers Team. As the call concluded, Susie cautiously asked Cathy if she would appreciate being
called by someone from the choir at First Church to give her more
information about their music ministry. After some hesitation, Cathy
responded, "Yes, I would like to know more about the choir, although
I am not sure that I am skilled enough to contribute much to that
group—they sounded so professional!" As the call concluded, Susie
once again expressed her appreciation for Bill and Cathy attending
worship, and she added her hope that Bill and Cathy might find a
church home at First Church.

Next Susie called Jennifer Rodriguez and began with the same opening statement. However, in this case she was interrupted by Jennifer
exclaiming, "I am right in the middle of feeding my children and I don't
have time to talk." Susie quickly responded, "I am sorry to have both-
ered you, and I will be glad to call back at a more convenient time. I
met you yesterday, and I know that your children are delightful and
energetic."

"Oh, you are the nice lady who spoke to me yesterday after worship," exclaimed Jennifer. "I am sorry that I didn't recognize your
voice. Yes, please call me later this evening after the kids are in bed—
maybe about 9:30." After quickly agreeing to that arrangement, Susie
ended the call. She had learned in the training not to force the issue
with newcomers, but to respect their privacy. And so at 9:30 PM she
called Jennifer again and found her ready to talk. In fact, Jennifer
talked for more than twenty minutes about her busy schedule, her work
as a waitress, her school, and her worries about neglecting her children.
Susie was such a good listener that Jennifer found it easy to talk to her,
and she even added this comment: "I am sorry I have rambled on, but
I am always glad to talk with an adult in the evening."

This phone call concluded without Susie asking any specific questions about church activities or involvement, and she also noted on the
profile of Jennifer: "Very busy young mother, lots of concerns for her
children. I am not sure a singles group is really the best way to involve
her."

After finishing her reports, Susie finally relaxed, took a deep breath, and uttered a brief prayer, "Thank you Lord for bringing these people to our church. Help us to know them better, so that we can respond well to their needs and help them to find a place at our church."

CHAPTER FIVE

Listening to Newcomers

Six weeks later the Newcomers Team had its usual meeting prior to its lunch with the church staff. This week brought the names of a few more first-time visitors to worship and the team planned an initial phone call response to those newcomers.

Then team members' conversation turned to the newcomers from the previous few months, and Jill shared the reports of their efforts to involve those newcomers in the life of the church. As she went through the list, she came to the names of three persons who had first been identified six weeks earlier: Bill and Cathy Johnson and Jennifer Rodriguez. "How are we doing at getting them involved in our church?" Jill asked.

The report was mixed. It noted that Bill Johnson had become quite involved in the men's Bible study and also in the SCORE group. It also noted that Cathy Johnson had initially attended choir practice for three weeks, and that she had sung with the choir one Sunday, but then she had not appeared again. This surprised the Newcomers Team, because they had been convinced that music was the way to help Cathy find her place at First Church.

The report on Jennifer Rodriguez was even more disappointing. She and her children had attended worship three times in the past six weeks, but Jennifer had not responded to the invitations for her to become involved in the new singles group at the church. *Her children had attended Sunday school on two of the Sundays they were present, but the Newcomers Team knew from their experience that it was important to get the parent involved in order to keep the children involved. Pastor Jones had often expressed this truth with the statement, "Not too many three-year-olds drive themselves to church."*

"Where have we missed it?" mused Jill. "We made the initial phone calls, and from the information on the profile we made sure that more invitations were extended. But somehow we have not adequately matched their needs/hopes/desires with our ministries at First Church." The Newcomers Team agreed to share these three names with the church staff, in order to discern together a better way to involve Bill and Cathy and Jennifer.

After listening to the concerns of the Newcomers Team about the three newcomers, Pastor Jones observed, "It sounds to me like we need to listen more carefully to these persons. Have we scheduled a listening visit with them yet?" The Newcomers Team members looked at one another somewhat chagrined, and replied, "I guess we were so sure we knew their profiles that we skipped that step." After a few smiles and shrugs all around, it was determined that a listening visit needed to be scheduled for the Johnsons and for Jennifer. After some further discussion, it was agreed that Pastor Jones should visit the Johnsons, and Jill should visit Jennifer.

* * *

LISTENING IS THE VITAL LINK

The relay team is approaching the anchor leg of the race. This is not the final lap, but it is the lap just before the final lap. It is known as the "anchor leg" of the race because it is the lap that can set up the team for the final lap and—one hopes—the run to victory. While the runner on the anchor leg is often not necessarily the fastest runner on the team, that person is usually the most adept at receiving and giving the baton. The one who runs this lap is often said to "anchor" the team, to prepare the team for victory.

The same is also true in the process of assimilating new disciples for Jesus Christ. The most crucial time in that assimilation
process is the time spent listening to the newcomer, which we
call the "listening visit." The listening visit is the "anchor" or
vital link between an early response and the movement toward
assimilation into a role, task, or group. Without the information
gathered during an effective listening visit, it is difficult to find
the appropriate niche for each newcomer. And without the care
displayed during the listening visit, there may not be sufficient
trust for the newcomer to respond to an invitation for participation when it is offered.

DEMONSTRATING CARE

Many important things must transpire when the listening visit
is done well. Significant information will be gathered that can be
passed on to facilitate supportive ministry that may be needed by
the newcomer. Important data about interests and talents can be
gathered and forwarded to those extending invitations for further
involvement. But the heart of the listening visit is offering the
newcomer an experience of genuine concern for them as a unique
person infinitely valuable to God. Listening is the anchor of a
dynamic, growing, supportive relationship.

The people in our lives who love us and care about us also regularly and genuinely listen to us. They ask about our lives and our
experiences. They listen to our opinions, our dreams, our hurts
and fears, our successes and failures. They want to know about us
so they ask and they listen. They demonstrate through their listening that we are important and valuable. One of the best ways
that they show their love is through such attentive listening.

Good listening centers on knowing and understanding the person we're listening to. Good listening uses open-ended questions
to give opportunity for newcomers to share their life experiences,
hopes, concerns, and gifts. The listening visit is not about our
sharing what a great church we have in order to "sell" the newcomer. Instead it is a way of discovering how our church can

connect with newcomers and their life issues. The old saying is true: people don't care about how much we know (even about our church, even about Jesus) until they know how much we care. The listening visit is pivotal to the process of assimilating new disciples.

HEARING THE LIFE TRANSITION EVENTS

A second important goal of the listening visit is to hear from the newcomer the stories of the life transition events that have occurred within the two months or so prior to him or her first beginning to look for a church home. Dean Hoge's insightful study of over two hundred Roman Catholic parishes sought to find out why persons first came to a new church.[1] His study revealed that more than 97 percent of newcomers had one or more life transition event occur in their lives two months prior to seeking the church (he called them "facilitating events"). A smaller study of United Methodists also researched why new-comers first came to a church.[2] This study of five churches of various sizes discovered that 100 percent of those newcomers also had life transition events occur prior to attendance.

The psychological principle highlighted in these two studies is unmistakable. People do not change their behavior without reason. One or more transitions in people's lives must motivate them to change their behavior and attend a church for the first time. Some of these transitions were exciting experiences: marriage, birth of a child, job promotion, moving to a larger or more comfortable home, graduation, and retirement. Other transitions were difficult experiences: divorce, death, illness, forced relocation, family conflict, job loss, and bankruptcy. All of these life transitions (even the happier ones) produce stress that causes the newcomer to seek support, guidance, and relationships of faith to better cope with the transitions. Sometimes newcomers understand the stressors behind their church search and other times they simply search for a church without connecting it to the life transition stressors they are experiencing.

The Bible is filled with examples of persons who either came to faith or found deeper faith out of a crisis in their lives: Jacob finally wrestled with God all night only after being chased and cornered by those he had cheated, Moses encountered God in the burning bush only after fleeing Egypt from a murder he had committed, Esther risked her own life in order to save the lives of her people when their survival was threatened, and Saul became Paul on the Damascus road following his participation in Stephen's execution. Faith is often and regularly born out of a life transition event that becomes a crisis. The more we can discover these life transition events during a listening visit with newcomers, the more we will be able to provide sensitive and appropriate ministry with them during these transitions.

This perspective can also change the way pastors look at the "Monday Morning News." Pastors often look at the reports on their desks on Monday morning (from the experiences of Sunday morning) to evaluate how things are progressing in their ministry. Included in that list of data might be the Sunday morning worship attendance, the Sunday school attendance, the amount of the offering, and perhaps a list of first-time visitors. From the perspective of understanding the impact of life transition events, it is important to see that the list of first-time visitors is a list of persons who have significant need for a prompt pastoral response of sensitivity, concern, and care.

DISCOVERING THE GIFTS AND TALENTS

A third goal of the listening visit with newcomers is to discover their gifts, talents, skills, interests, and passions. This information will be vital in helping them find a place of connection and spiritual growth within the life of the congregation. Too often churches try to fill "empty slots." These attempts rarely result in making a good connection for the newcomer and instead are often experienced as puzzling and alienating. When invitations to involvement show little concern or understanding for who the newcomer is, then they remind the newcomer how little the church really knows her or has helped her to belong. But when invitations to involvement are rooted in an understanding of the newcomer's gifts and talents that is the result of active and caring listening, those invitations are gratefully received and often responded to with enthusiasm.

One story from the early ministry (before he knew the importance of listening visits) of one pastor may illustrate: A young couple visited the small church where the pastor was serving. He greeted them after worship for several Sundays and enjoyed those brief conversations. Then the young couple stopped attending for several weeks. Due to busyness and ignorance and inexperience, the pastor did not follow up with them to listen to them. A few weeks later, this same pastor was visiting with a neighboring pastor who shared enthusiastically about a new young couple who were attending the small church that he served. Soon the first pastor discovered they were the same couple who had attended his church several weeks earlier. Courageously asking if the young couple had said anything about their first church experience, the second pastor replied, "As a matter of fact, they did. They said your church was friendly and there were a lot of nice people, but no one asked them to get involved. So they started attending my church and now they are helping out as youth counselors." The first pastor was stunned. He had potential youth workers under his nose and lost them because he didn't listen and didn't ask how they would like to serve. That pastor learned the hard way about the importance of listening. Newcomers want to get involved where their gifts, talents, and interests are, if we will give them the opportunity after finding our what fits them well.

Not all newcomers want to be youth counselors, of course, but all newcomers want to have an opportunity to be involved in helping serve and do ministry in the church. All newcomers have gifts, talents, interests, and skills to bring to ministry that have been given to them by God. Those differ, so it is critical that we as the church discover the unique combination of ministry assets individual newcomers have in order to help them grow and develop as disciples of Jesus Christ. Then our invitations for involvement can be an outgrowth of our compassionate listening to those newcomers.

Who can make such a listening visit? The pastor might make listening visits. (We have made hundreds of such visits and enjoy the enthusiasm and conversation with newcomers.) However, these listening visits can also be made by trained laypersons (in teams of two), and they can be equally effective in gathering needed information and building relationships. The important factor is that a person is trained to listen and is clear about the objectives of a listening visit.

SETTING UP THE LISTENING VISIT: THE PHONE CALL

The process begins with a phone call to the newcomer to arrange for a listening visit. Gone are the days when you can simply stop by for a visit and be confident that the party will be at home. So it is recommended that you phone in advance of your visit. The caller might say something like this: "Good evening, Terry. This is John Smith from Trinity Church. I'm calling you to arrange a time when I might come to your home to listen and visit with you and your spouse in order to get better acquainted with you and your family. I would like to come next Tuesday evening at seven thirty and visit for about forty-five minutes, if that is convenient for the two of you.... Great! I'll see you next Tuesday at seven thirty. Good to talk with you. Goodbye." (If another person will be coming with you on the listening visit, that information needs to be shared during the phone call so there is no surprise at the door.) The important word to use in making this phone call is *listen* because that accurately describes your intent, and because it sounds less threatening than phrases like "We want to share with you," which may connote selling the church to them.

An increasing number of persons are resistant about people coming into their homes, so those making the listening visit need to be flexible, not only with the time but also with the location.

It is still preferable to make a listening visit in the home but sometimes it is necessary to meet at the church, a restaurant, or some other neutral location in order to make the listening visit happen at all. Making the visit is more important than its location. So do your best to negotiate a convenient time and place in order to listen to the newcomer for the purpose of building relationships and gathering needed data for ministry follow-up and assimilation into the life of the congregation.

BEGINNING THE LISTENING VISIT

The key to beginning the listening visit well is to let your behavior demonstrate that you will not be pushy in your approach. Some newcomers are fearful that you may be coming to manipulate them or to sell the church, as other religious groups sometimes do. So when the newcomer answers the door, restate the agreement you reached on the phone—why you're here (to listen and get acquainted with this person and his family) and how long you anticipate visiting (up to forty-five minutes). This is important because the person you spoke to on the phone may not be the same person who answers the door. By restating why you're here and checking to see if it is still convenient to visit, it also communicates that you are not coming to push your way through the door to sell the church.

Once you are invited inside, don't take your coat off until invited to do so. Don't move into another room until invited. Don't sit until you are offered a seat. Your behavior should say to the newcomer that you're not interested in taking over, but rather in relating and responding to this person as a guest. This will help the newcomer relax and be more at ease, and more receptive and responsive during the conversation. If a choice of location is offered, the kitchen table is a great place for conversation. Try to find a seating arrangement that makes it easy for the newcomer to talk and share with you about his life, which is an important goal of a listening visit.

Look around the room for objects that that can be conversation starters. Ask about pictures on display, because those may open conversation about family and significant experiences. Remark about trophies, decorative objects, and furniture, any of which might give insight into hobbies, interests, and talents. People display these in their homes as a way of expressing themselves. To ignore these items is to discount not only what they value but also to discount them as persons. This opening chat about the house and its displays may open up possibilities for further, significant conversation later in the visit.

YOUR LISTENING SKILLS

The listening visit will be greatly enhanced if you use good listening skills. Chief among those listening skills is the art of asking good questions, especially open-ended questions. This is a question that cannot be answered with a simple yes or no, but rather invites the person to share further. Open-ended questions that might be helpful in a listening visit include the following: "Tell me about your family" or "What is special about each member of your family?" or "How long have you lived in the community?" or "What do you like best about this community?" or "Where do you work?" Each of these questions will open up possibilities for further questions to facilitate the newcomer sharing about personal experiences and values. Although a listening visit is a conversation that we share with the newcomer, it is more like an interview in that the newcomer does most of the talking and the person visiting does most of the listening.

Another helpful listening skill is the "check for feeling," which identifies the feeling being expressed by the newcomer (usually through body language and tone of voice) and then asks for confirmation if the feeling is correct. For example, the check for feeling might be, "It sounds like you are excited about your new job, is that right?" ("excited" is the feeling word) or "It seems like you are lonely in this new community without your old friends, is that true?" ("lonely" is the feeling word). The check for feeling lets the newcomer know that you're listening not only to what she says, but also to her feelings, which gives energy to the conversation and allows the newcomer to share more deeply than she otherwise would. Such a check for feeling always ends in a question, because we are not being amateur psychiatrists; we are listening and asking the question for better understanding.

Another helpful skill in listening is paraphrasing. Paraphrasing is not simply parroting back what is said, but rather it is a rephrasing of what we heard. This enables the person sharing to know that the listener not only is listening but also is seeking to understand. Paraphrasing therefore not only helps clarify the conversation but also affirms that the person sharing is worth understanding. Paraphrasing can also enable the person visiting to respond to what is currently being said until he or she can form a question that concretely moves the conversation forward.

It may be helpful to remember some practical tips to use in the listening visit. It is easier for persons to talk about the past than the present so you might want to start the conversation in the past and focus on past history with your earlier questions like, "When did you first come to this town?" Another suggestion is to start with facts and experiences and then later move to recognizing feelings. Also remember that family, house, health, and jobs are good early subjects for conversation (since they are also topics that often encompass life transitions events, which is one key area of the newcomer's life you hope to learn more about during the listening visit). Then you can eventually move to a discussion about interests, hobbies, and the church.

DISCOVERING THEIR INTERESTS AND TALENTS

After ample time for the newcomers to share about their lives and time for you to listen for the life transition events that have occurred (especially within the last few months), the conversation might move toward a discussion of the church. You can begin that part of the conversation by asking questions about any past church experience they may have had, exploring both positive experiences they may wish to have again and negative experiences they may want to avoid. This sharing can give you valuable insight into what they are looking for in their new church.

You can also explore what ministries they may have been involved with in a former church. This can be very important information for finding out where the newcomers might fit well into the life of your congregation. In the listening visit, one of the goals is to discover connection points where the newcomer may have interests, skills, talents, gifts, and passions that can be used within the life of the church. One of the best ways to discover this about newcomers is to simply ask them! What did they do well in their last church? What did they enjoy doing and find fulfillment from (which may give a clue as to their spiritual gifts)? What did they not do well or enjoy or gain fulfillment from? It is also helpful to know what interests, talents, skills, gifts, and passions are not of interest to the newcomer.

If the newcomers have not had significant church experience, then the same questions can be phrased more generally to help identify their interests, talents, skills, gifts, and passions. "What do you enjoy doing? What do you like to do in your spare time? What are you good at? What do you do that gives you a sense of achievement and fulfillment?" All of these point to possible connections within the life of the church. They are also good questions for those with significant church experience, because not all gifts, talents, interests, skills, and passions are utilized within the life of the church. Some are first and best expressed outside the church. So ask about talents, interests, and gifts there as well, too! After all, ministry is not confined to the bounds of the church.

ENDING THE LISTENING VISIT

By now we hope that your listening visit has gone extremely well. Through your questions and checks for feelings, you have recognized a couple of life transition events that occurred to the newcomer within the last few months. You have developed significant trust with the newcomer and have begun to build a relationship you are looking forward to continuing in the church. You are excited about the interests, talents, and gifts that the newcomer has and have some thoughts about how the newcomer might use those resources to connect well within the life of the congregation. And you have even resisted the temptation to invite the new-comer to a few of those opportunities. Instead you responded to the person's inquiries about choir and a Sunday school class with a promise to have someone from those areas of ministry contact them later with further information. Over forty minutes have passed since you arrived. It is time to end this listening visit, but how can you bring this visit to an appropriate close?

One helpful insight is based on the same principle you used when you first arrived at the newcomer's door. Use your body lan-guage and behavior to signal that you are leaving (the same way you used behavior and body language to signal when you arrived that you were coming to be a guest). Lean forward in your seat so it is clear that you are ready to get up. You might then summarize briefly what you have heard and any information you have prom-ised to get back to him with. Ask if he would like to close with prayer. If so, make it positive, affirming, and brief by thanking God for new friends, a chance to share together, and praying for God's guidance through our transitions and in the life of our church.

If the newcomer drops a new, significant topic of conversation as you are leaving (which is not unusual if the listening visit was well received), you have a choice. You can let the person know that you care about what he is saying but you do not have time now to continue and would be open to schedule another time for further conversation. Or you can renegotiate to stay another ten to fifteen minutes to continue the discussion. Either choice is acceptable, depending on your schedule that evening. But after that time is up, it is time to go. So shake hands, exchange good-byes, and leave.

As you walk back to your car, do not converse with your part-ner and it is especially important that you do not laugh (usually due to releasing nervous tension after making the visit). The newcomer will be watching and wondering what you are saying about him, or worse, he will be wondering why you are laughing at him. All of the care shown in the visit can then be negated as you walk right down the driveway! Instead, get in the car, drive several blocks away from the house, and then debrief the visit and write down the pertinent information about the newcomer for follow-up and assimilation.

CONCLUSION

The listening visit is indeed the "anchor" in our efforts to help newcomers connect with the congregation. By demonstrating our care through careful listening, by discovering the ministry needs amid the life transition events, and by hearing of the talents, gifts, skills, interest, and passions of the newcomers, we are ready to help connect them in meaningful participation and relationships within the church. And all of this is facilitated by the effective listening visit. It anchors and provides stability to our whole assimilation process. Newcomers need the assurance of that kind of stability—knowing that we in the church will be there for them, providing care, listening, and helping them to deal with their life transitions.

Listening communicates our love and our caring. One might even go so far as to submit that listening is a true form of love. Reflect on this as you read a unique adaptation of Paul's Letter to the Corinthians about love and listening that we have used:

> [Listening] is patient and kind; [listening] is not jealous or boastful; it is not arrogant or rude. [Listening] does not insist on its own way; it is not irritable or resentful; it does not rejoice at wrong, but rejoices in the right. [Listening] bears all things, believes all things, hopes all things, endures all things. [Listening] never ends.
>
> 1 Corinthians 13:4-8*a* (RSV)

Soon it will be time to hand off the baton for the next leg of the relay race of newcomer assimilation. One hopes that the listening visit has provided the anchor leg to this continuing race.

* * *

As she approached the door of Jennifer's apartment, Jill was a bit nervous. Although she had made numerous listening visits, this was her first solo visit. However, when she had difficulty finding a partner from their listening visitor training to accompany her, Jill had determined that visiting with Jennifer alone might actually be better, especially since Jennifer was single.

The visit went well. After reminding Jennifer at the doorway that she was there to visit and to listen, Jill received a warm welcome. Her two children were already in bed (which was why Jennifer had chosen this somewhat later time of the evening for a visit). After some initial conversation during which Jill commented on the many beautiful photos of her children and the refrigerator covered with the children's drawings and projects, Jennifer proudly told Jill about her children. She also shared the whole story of her early marriage, its breakup, and her present struggles to raise her children while working and attending school. Jill was easily able to use her check-for-feeling listening skill and to empathize with Jennifer by saying, "It certainly sounds like you feel a bit overwhelmed at times." This deepened their conversation, with Jennifer able to share her pain and loneliness with Jill who responded with care and compassion.

Not far into the conversation, Jill found herself thinking, "No wonder we have not found the right niche for Jennifer. We have been dealing with her as a single young woman, but her real needs have to do with her children." In fact, over and over again, Jennifer talked about how much she hated the term single mother and how she feared that she might not be raising her children properly. Hearing that opening, Jill offered a suggestion: "We have a wonderful young moms group at the church, where we provide childcare for the kids and the young mothers are able to talk about issues of child-rearing. They sometimes have a speaker or a book study on topics related to raising children, but mostly it is a supportive group of young moms dealing with those same issues. Would it be all right if I asked one of those young mothers to call and invite you to their group?"

Jennifer's response—immediately nodding her head and the tears rushing to her eyes—was a definite "Yes!" to that suggestion. After a nice visit of about thirty-five minutes, including sharing some herbal tea, Jill offered to pray for Jennifer and her children. Jennifer shyly confessed, "I grew up Catholic, but I guess I never really learned how to pray. But I do talk to God a lot about my children." Jill responded compassionately and warmly by sharing some of her own growth in comfort with prayer, and then offered a lovely prayer for Jennifer and her children. The two women actually hugged briefly at the door before Jill departed.

Driving home and thinking about the visit, Jill was grateful that she had taken the time to listen to Jennifer's story. "Now," said Jill aloud to herself in the car, "we can finally help Jennifer find a home in our church. I'm going to call Colleen Damsky from the young moms group, and ask her to invite Jennifer to their next gathering."

* * *

On that same evening, Pastor Jones visited with Bill and Cathy. It proved to be a difficult visit, requiring all of the pastor's best listening skills. The visit was pleasant enough, but Bill kept dominating the conversation, talking about how much he enjoyed the men's group and his subsequent involvement in their SCORE project. Pastor Jones noticed that Bill's animated conversation seemed to be avoiding deeper issues. Using the check-for-feelings skill, the pastor asked Cathy, "You seem more quiet during these discussions about church activities, and so I am wondering if you have felt more lonely and isolated during this move to the city?"

That question, with its invitation to talk about her feelings on a deeper level, opened up the rest of the conversation allowing Cathy to share her real fears and hurts. Admitting that she enjoyed music but was intimidated by the large, nearly professional choir at First Church was just the beginning. After Pastor Jones nodded sympathetically and admitted to being "musically challenged," Cathy then proceeded to talk about her loneliness, how much she missed her friends back in Middleton, and how much she had relied upon their support during her tough times. Pastor Jones patiently listened, paraphrased a few of her comments, and waited for the right moment to ask more about those tough times.

After continuing to listen carefully, Pastor Jones then asked the open-ended question that allowed Cathy to share the rest of her story: "You mentioned the support you enjoyed with friends in Middleton during your tough times. Can you tell me a little more about those tough times and the support you received?" Tears came to Cathy's eyes, and Bill lowered his head sadly, as Cathy recounted her yearlong struggle with breast cancer three years ago. She talked warmly (and this was the time when her smile was the brightest) about the women choir members from Middleton who brought meals, visited her in the hospital, prayed with her, and helped her through those tough times. Pastor Jones allowed this whole story to unfold, and then asked about her current health (which Cathy said was fine) and about her hopes for the future.

The listening visit with the Johnsons revealed to Pastor Jones that the assimilation issues for Cathy would revolve around support, care, prayer, and finding new friends. Bill seemed to be finding that kind of support through the men's group and especially through his involvement in SCORE (Bill had talked most enthusiastically about his joy in helping Kareem Thomas to get his new business up and going), but Cathy had not found that kind of support through the large adult choir at First Church. While some folks in that choir were friends and supportive in smaller groupings, the choir as a whole was large, "nearly professional" as Cathy had said, often sang with the city's symphony, and was not the type of smaller, close-knit choir that had been so supportive of Cathy in Middleton. After listening to that whole story, Pastor Jones offered Cathy another option to consider. "You know, our large adult choir at the eleven o'clock service is not our only musical group. We also have a small women's ensemble that practices twice a month and sings once a month in the early service. That group of women is one of the most supportive, prayerful groups we have in our church. In fact, some of the women say that they are really a prayer group that also happens to sing. Would you give me permission to suggest your name to Kyle Overstreet, our music director, so that he might call you sometime and talk about the ensemble?" Cathy hesitated, looked at her husband Bill for confirmation, and then said, "That sounds more like something that I would enjoy—if Bill could get up and go to the early service with me." After receiving her husband's strong assurance,

Cathy smiled again and said, "Thank you for understanding. I guess it is just harder for me to start over in a new city and new church than it is for some other people—like my husband."

As their time drew to a close, and Pastor Jones asked about having a closing prayer, Bill blurted out, "We have another prayer request, Pastor. It looks like our daughter Sarah may be moving back home with us. She has been living with a guy, and that relationship isn't working, she's lost her job, and so we may have her back home again with us. Would you pray for Sarah, too?"

Hearing such a large issue dropped at the end of a listening visit did not surprise Pastor Jones, who quickly negotiated to stay a little longer, past the forty-five minutes they had set, in order to hear more about Sarah. That extra time of listening was another important demonstration of the kind of caring and support that the Johnsons could find at First Church.

On the way home from visiting the Johnsons, Pastor Jones was reminded, once again, of how important—really essential—it was to listen to newcomers like the Johnsons. Otherwise, the church would never have known how to properly assimilate and include them into the life of the congregation. Meanwhile, the Johnsons were also debriefing the visit, and Cathy announced to her husband, Bill, "For the first time since we moved here, I really believe that we may have found a church home."

including Newcomers

T his Monday morning's meeting of the Newcomers Team was a busy one. In addition to planning their initial responses to several first-time visitors to worship, the team also dealt with the information they had received from the listening visits to the Johnsons and to Jennifer Rodriguez. Jill reported personally on her visit with Jennifer and her discovery that things like the singles group would not really respond to Jennifer's needs. She shared her suggestion about the young moms group, and the Newcomers Team readily agreed to that idea.

Then Jill shared the written report from Pastor Jones about the Johnsons. Although the report was worded carefully to protect confidentiality outside the Newcomers Team, it was clear from the suggestions listed that the Johnsons also needed a different approach for being included into the life of First Church. The group agreed to ask Kyle Overstreet to speak with Cathy about the women's ensemble group.

As the meeting of the Newcomers Team closed and the members prepared to join the rest of the church staff for lunch to talk more about these assimilation issues, Jill thanked the team members for their fine work. She also reminded them: "We are in the homestretch with Jennifer and with Bill and Cathy. If we can help them to become more fully assimilated into and included in the congregation, then I think we will really make a difference in their lives and in the life of this church."

Steve responded with one more of his favorite sayings. "Yes," he said, "if we can help people belong, then they will join."

Jill cautioned the group to keep its focus on welcoming newcomers by including and involving them in the ministries of the church. And then she added, "And yes, Steve, you are right. People who really belong to our church will likely join as members too. When that happens, then it will be a great celebration of our life together."

* * *

THE FINAL LAP

Ultimately it all comes down to the final leg, initiated by the final handoff. It is especially important for this handoff to be clean, smooth, and in stride. The timing between the runner entering the exchange zone and the last runner receiving the baton can mean the difference between winning and losing. As the last runner takes the baton in full stride, the team heads toward the tape marking the end of the race.

The same is true of our relay race of assimilating newcomers. In too many churches the "baton" of connecting with newcomers is fumbled and dropped at this point in the process of assimilation. Sometimes the problem is that the one participating in the listening visit does not immediately recognize the newcomer's needs, and, thus, fails to invite the newcomer to participate in groups that can be significant places of belonging for the newcomer. The timing of those invitations is also critical, and sometimes the opportunity is lost. When the assimilation team completes the handoff cleanly, when the listening becomes inviting, which then becomes connecting, which, in turn, becomes discipling—well, then, everyone wins!

Let's rehearse the whole process of assimilation: Attracting newcomers enables us to create awareness so newcomers might visit our church. Welcoming newcomers with hospitality is important when they arrive to visit the church. Responding well to newcomers after the visit makes a difference in the newcomers' experience that can lead to return visits. Listening well to newcomers helps us identify potential ministry opportunities and places to connect them within the life of the church. But all of this effort will bear little fruit without a consistent network of invitation that connects these newcomers with groups and ministries in the life of the church. Let's examine further this assimilation/invitation process, some models for doing this assimilation/invitation, and also some principles about how to employ this network in your own process of assimilating newcomers.

THE GOAL IS BELONGING

There is wisdom in Stephen Covey's book *The Seven Habits of Highly Effective People* that we must "begin with the end in mind."[1] The "end" for the relay race of assimilation is belonging. The "tape" that we are straining toward is helping newcomers belong or connect with the church in a meaningful way. That is the focal point of our assimilation process. We are working to have newcomers belong to a ministry team, a small group, a task force, or a class. You may be wondering why "belonging" is our goal, rather than "membership" or "joining." The next chapter will make it clear that "joining" is a celebration of the fact that a newcomer already "belongs" to our church. For us, this is an important theological point: we do not focus upon assimilating newcomers just to make them into church members to support our institution. Rather, we focus upon assimilating newcomers to meet their needs and to help them to find a place of belonging in the body of Christ.

Most newcomers are seeking a place to belong, but this is particularly true of younger adults, those under the age of forty. Leonard Sweet reminds us in his book *Post-modern Pilgrims* that one of the keys to ministry with these younger adults is helping them make relational connections.[2] Newcomers need to connect and belong to the church. In a smaller church, newcomers belong to the whole church because it functions like one big family. In larger churches (over one hundred in average attendance), newcomers must belong to a group within the church. That group is where they are known, connected, can serve, find care, and develop meaningful and supportive relationships. Assimilation is connecting people into a meaningful, supportive, caring group.

In fact, this issue of belonging is so important that 75 percent of newcomers decide within ninety days if the church they have visited will become the church they continue to be a part of. Newcomers evaluate if this church will become "our" church by whether or not this church becomes a place where they genuinely belong and feel at home. So our assimilation as a church needs to be intentional, steady, hospitable, and immediate.

This final leg of the assimilation relay race means taking the clues we gained from the listening visit and using those clues to help the newcomer develop bonds of connection. After discovering the newcomer's life transition events, interests, gifts, talents, skills, and passions, the church must extend appropriate invitations to form relationships of belonging. Making "invitation" the center of the assimilation process is a vital and necessary shift of strategy and style for many churches that can result in newcomers connecting to the church and to the Lord of the church.

FROM INFORMATIONAL TO INVITATIONAL CULTURE

There is a key transition in thinking and behavior that needs to occur in order to expand the effectiveness of our assimilating newcomers into the life and ministry of the church. We must realize that simply informing people about opportunities to participate is not adequate to guide and inspire most newcomers into participation and involvement. Whether the information comes through bulletins, newsletters, pulpit announcements, sign-up sheets, or general invitations to come and be a part, most newcomers will not leap into participating, getting involved, or connecting simply because they read or heard about the opportunity to do so. Information is an important part of communicating that can lead to involvement, but it is not enough if that is all that is done.

We must go beyond informing; the church must focus on inviting people to participate, especially around their gifts, passions, skills, talents, and abilities. This change in style from merely informing to specifically inviting will be helpful and immediately relevant in several ministry areas within the life of the church, but especially in newcomer assimilation.

DEVELOPING THE NETWORK

Now that we've clarified the importance of inviting newcomers to participate, we can now explore the process for developing this key network for assimilating newcomers. The key principle in developing this network is to start simple and keep it simple. A good system generally should not be too complex to maintain, nor should we be endlessly searching for the perfect process so most of the effort is used up in the design and tinkering rather than in implementing and ministering. It is essential that this newcomer assimilation process is kept simple enough to be consistent (doing the assimilation for all the newcomers not just a select few) and constant (doing this assimilation all the time, not just periodically).

Developing this network begins with identifying all the groups currently available in the life of the church in which a newcomer could easily become a part of and be welcomed. This could include Sunday school classes, Bible studies, women's circles, men's groups, athletic teams, choirs, musical groups, ministry teams, or task forces. For each of these groups, a group host must be identified and recruited (better still, two hosts, perhaps one of each gender). This host is a person who is able and excited to extend a personal invitation to a newcomer in a welcoming way. The host helps welcome the newcomer into the group and initiates connection with others in the group without "smothering" or pushing the newcomer. Obviously this host is often not the group leader, but rather another person (or team of two persons) whose sole focus is on inviting and welcoming newcomers to the group.

The church then develops a whole network of groups that are open to newcomers, and also a network of good hosts who can invite and help newcomers to connect with individual groups. The church can also expand the network by helping other existing groups to become open to newcomers by discovering good hosts. And most important, the church can also expand its capacity to assimilate newcomers by continuing to develop new groups, classes, ministry teams, and task forces. In fact, it is important to develop at least one new group every eighteen to twenty-four months so that newcomers have an opportunity to be part of a group in which members do not already have a long history together. Groups with a long history tend to feel closed to newcomers.

It is critical to the assimilation process for these groups not only to assist in providing a place for newcomers to belong but also to assist in helping those who participate in the group to grow in their relationship with Jesus Christ. Such participation then not only connects newcomers to others in the group in meaningful ways but also connects them to Christ. So the softball team, for example, not only enjoys playing together and developing camaraderie but also takes time for a devotional that talks about spiritual issues like teamwork in serving God, shares personal joys and concerns, and prays together. This newcomer assimilation network works best when it helps form not only friendship but also faith.

FINDING THE SPONSORS

Another part of the network of inviting/assimilating newcomers is the person we call the sponsor. The best way to describe the role and function of the newcomer sponsor is to remember the old-fashioned switchboard operator. The sponsor receives vital information from the listening team about the newcomer, notes the potential connecting points of the newcomer's life transitions with the potential opportunities within the groups and ministries of the church, and then helps connect with the host of the appropriate group on behalf of the newcomer so that the host to the group can invite the newcomer. Sponsors keep the communication flowing so that newcomers can become connected, which is what switchboard operators once did for phone callers. Sponsors are persons who want to help newcomers get connected, so they stay in touch with newcomers (perhaps as informal greeters on Sunday morning) and are visible in welcoming newcomers.

EXTENDING THE INVITATION

Once the sponsor has contacted the host, it is time to extend the invitation to the newcomer. This is done face-to-face or by telephone call, because a personal contact is the relational way to invite. The newcomer is invited to come to the class, group, ministry, or task that is based on the gifts, skills, talents, interests, or passions of the newcomer. It is even better if the person extending the invitation already has a positive relationship with the newcomer. It takes effort and intentionality to handle the invitation well.

Why go through all of this anyway? Why not just have the person doing the listening visit offer the invitation to the choir or Sunday school class or softball team? After all, the person making the listening visit knows about each of these opportunities for involvement and when the newcomer can link up to participate. Why not just have this person invite the newcomer when the connecting point becomes obvious during the listening visit? Why bring the host into this process? Isn't it easier and more direct to just invite the newcomer during the listening visit?

The answer is significant and is also a specific example of what it means to shift from being an informing congregational culture to an inviting congregational culture. The listening visitor can only inform about the group or activity; that person cannot invite, even if you describe the act of informing the newcomer as "inviting." A real invitation can only be offered to a newcomer by someone who is participating in the group. Invitations are always relational—extended by someone who will be there if the newcomer comes to the group, class, ministry, or activity. Eighty percent of Americans classify themselves as shy rather than outgoing.[3] Therefore most newcomers are unlikely to initiate going to a group or ministry where they do not know anyone. Simply being informed about the group by a nonparticipant will not be effective.

If, instead, a host of the group extends the invitation, then the newcomer knows at least one person who will be at the group when the newcomer arrives and that person will probably help the newcomer feel welcomed. The host will greet the newcomer when he arrives and will also introduce him to others in the group and help him feel at home and connected with the group. The host will provide hospitality without overwhelming or pressuring the newcomer when he comes. Only a person who is part of the group can invite a newcomer to come, and when a newcomer knows at least one person there, he is far more likely to come.

Our example here is Jesus. He did not simply inform his potential disciples that they should attend a meeting. Instead he went to where they were and personally invited them to "come and follow me." He saw in them the possibility of using their gifts and skills (fishing) to be part of this new religious movement (fishers of persons). And as they responded, he was there to greet them, train them, and help them connect with the other disciples and with God. His method was no general announcement to whomever; no sign-up sheet or newsletter plea. It was personal, relational, and hospitable. It was a genuine invitation to come. And the disciples came. We need to go and do likewise with each newcomer; extend the invitation to come and connect with our group and with God.

FOLLOW-UP AND ACCOUNTABILITY

The sponsor gives the newcomer's name, phone number, and pertinent information to the host of the appropriate group or ministry so the invitation can be offered. This invitation is planned carefully to help the newcomer find the right place to belong in the life of the church and to begin connecting with the group. Then it is essential for the sponsor to check back with the host to make sure the invitation has actually been extended to the newcomer and to see if the newcomer came to that ministry or group. Accountability and support need to be provided to the host by the sponsor.

If this invitation does not result in the desired connection for the newcomer, the sponsor needs to know so he or she can reflect further on what the listening team shared about the newcomer and seek another potential group or ministry where the newcomer might belong. This "switchboard operator" (sponsor) then contacts the host of that other group or ministry so its host can extend a new invitation to a potential place of belonging. This process is repeated until a connection is made or the newcomer indicates that it is time to stop inviting. Again, the finish line toward which the assimilation team is racing is finding a place of belonging for the newcomer. Until that occurs or the newcomer indicates it's time to do otherwise, we keep going, consistently and constantly.

The sponsor also checks on the newcomer about once a month for at least the first three to six months to see how the newcomer is experiencing church. The sponsor can also ask if there is anything else the church can do to be helpful, or answer any other questions about the church and its opportunities. The newcomer can then indicate that there's no need for anymore invitations for a while. The newcomer can also ask about specific ministries and programs, to which the sponsor can ask permission to pass along these questions to a member of the group or ministry who is better able to answer. This sets the stage for the sponsor to contact the group host to answer the newcomer's questions and extend an invitation to the group if it then seems appropriate. It is still true that one of the best ways to find out how else we can help the newcomer is ask. Sponsors help the invitations occur and help newcomers belong.

CONNECTING WITH BALANCE

Initially, our goal for assimilating the newcomers who visit us is to help them connect with a ministry team, class, task, or group. Ultimately, our goal is to help them also be balanced in their connection with Jesus Christ and the church. To accomplish this requires balance in our belonging—whether we are a newcomer or a longtime member. An analogy may help to clarify this balance. In order to be in good health physically, we know that we need proper diet and exercise. The same is true with our spiritual life. We need to be fed through a group that provides care, Bible study, and prayer. We also need to exercise our gifts and talents by being involved in a ministry team. As we assimilate newcomers and extend invitations to them for involvement, our goal is to help them connect with both a place to be nurtured and with a place to do ministry. In this way, the newcomer is being assimilated as a new disciple with a balance between "being fed" and "exercising." Such balance is consistent with being connected with Christ, which is our ultimate goal.

CONCLUSION

We need to be consistent and constant in our efforts of assimilating newcomers. No newcomer is overlooked or forgotten. No newcomer is to be left behind in our care and concern. All newcomers are invited and included. The goal is to help them belong, connecting the newcomer with the church family and with the living Christ—the same Christ who never leaves us or forgets us. As the newcomers are connected to a group and to Christ, we are ready to celebrate that we have broken the tape and reached our goal as an assimilation team. But we are not yet finished. We will soon be ready to take the victory lap. That lap is membership. Once the newcomer belongs, then we can focus on his or her joining. Membership is not the goal of the race of assimilation; connecting with the church and with Christ is our goal. Membership is the victory lap we will celebrate because we have

broken the tape and won the victory of helping all newcomers
know that they belong.

* * *

*The reports back to the Newcomers Team were encouraging.
Colleen Damsky, the host from the young moms group, had called
Jennifer Rodriguez on the phone and after some hesitancy Jennifer had
attended that group twice already. Apparently, from the reports that
Jill had received from Colleen, Jennifer's son Sammy had been a real
hit with the young moms group too. That group included some play-
time for the children separate from their mothers, and also some
mutual experience with moms and kids together. Sammy had been his
usual entertaining self, and Jennifer was pleased to see her son find
such a nice group too. Jill sighed and exclaimed, "Wow! We were sure
off the mark when we tried to invite Jennifer to singles groups; it is
obvious now that the young moms group much better meets her
needs."*

*The report on Cathy Johnson was equally encouraging. As planned,
Kyle had been dispatched to visit with Cathy about the church's entire
music program and to invite her to participate in the women's ensemble. That group was small and much more intimate, and it seemed to
be less intimidating for Cathy. In fact, Kyle reported that at Cathy's
first rehearsal with the group she had started to gravitate toward her
host, Bessie Smith, in a way that obviously had to do with more than
their shared musical interests. Jill smiled as she heard this report. She
had been the one to recommend Bessie for Cathy's host, because she
was aware of Bessie's own battle with cancer many years ago. Jill had
kept confidential Pastor Jones's report about Cathy's struggle with
breast cancer, but she used that information in recommending Bessie
as the right choice to be Cathy's host. Apparently that connection was
working out very well.*

*"How about Bill Johnson?" Steve asked. "It is great to hear that his
wife, Cathy, is feeling more of a sense of belonging. But let's not overlook Bill."*

*"You are right," said Pastor Jones as the staff joined the Newcomers
Team for lunch. "And you will be happy to know that Bill is not only
involved in the SCORE group, he has also agreed over breakfast this*

morning to serve on our board of trustees next year. Clyde, thanks for the tip that Bill was very involved with the trustees at their last church." Clyde smiled proudly, and his wife Norma looked with admiration at Pastor Jones who always seemed to remember to thank the members of the Newcomers Team—and everyone else in the congregation for that matter—for their help with ministry. Norma thought to herself, "How does Pastor Jones do it? Always remembering to say thanks to volunteers like us!"

Another person feeling gratitude was Jill, who led the Newcomers Team. The team had worked hard to help Jennifer Rodriguez and Bill and Cathy Johnson find places of belonging at First Church. And now, Jill anticipated that this sense of belonging might pave the way for them to become members too.

CHAPTER SEVEN

Including Newcomers as New Members

The Newcomers Team was getting ready for the upcoming membership class. After carefully reviewing the attendance and participation patterns of several newcomers, the team members had selected about a dozen individuals to invite to this quarter's class. It had been their experience that newcomers who joined their church at a certain level of participation tended to maintain that same level of participation once they were official members. So, it was important not to invite newcomers to join until those persons really did belong and were active participants in the life of the church.

Current belief about participation levels ran counter to the previous style of conducting membership classes at First Church. Many years ago, if someone attended worship only once she or he might well be invited to come to a membership class in the hopes that "if they join, then they will become more active." It had been Pastor Jones who led the church leadership to rethink that process. Pastor Jones's own experience in the business world had led to the conclusion that all new members join with a certain "contract" or "covenant" about their membership. If the church encouraged and allowed persons to join who were minimally active, then that seemed to form a "contract" that affirmed such minimal participation. Indeed, Pastor Jones had struggled with getting longtime members who were relatively inactive to

think about becoming more active. "It is like getting someone to renegotiate his or her contract," observed Pastor Jones. "And that is not
easy to do. So let's make sure that any future membership classes are
filled with persons who are already active participants in the church."

That new philosophy had actually proved to be effective and quite
compatible with the Newcomers Team's emphasis upon helping newcomers belong. It had led to the saying (often quoted by Steve): "If we
can help people belong, then they will join."

As the Newcomers Team members prepared the finishing touches
for the membership class, they were sure to include the newcomers'
sponsors in the class, so that all newcomers arrived to find their sponsors present to help them feel at ease. The sponsors also had proved to
be an invaluable tool in translating the ideals of the membership class
into the reality of participation and belonging. It was one thing to talk
about church membership, but the sponsors helped to provide the practice applications of that concept.

Another aspect of the membership class that had become quite popu-
lar and effective was the way Pastor Jones led the entire class—including the sponsors, the newcomers, and any staff present—in a time of
sharing each individual's own faith journey. In fact, most people
reported that the best things about the membership class were the opportunities to hear and be encouraged by the faith stories of others, and
having their own opportunities to reflect upon God's activity in their
lives. Somehow Pastor Jones was able to make the membership class a
time for spiritual growth, not just a time for joining an institution.

"One more thing we haven't covered," said Jill as she looked at their
plans. "Who is going to bring the refreshments for the first session?"
All heads turned toward Susie who was notorious for making healthy
yet yummy desserts. It did not take much arm-twisting for Susie to
"volunteer" to bring refreshments for the first session.

* * *

THE VICTORY LAP

The tape is broken; the race is completed. Now the victory
celebration can begin. It's time for all the members of the team to

join hands and circle the track with arms raised to the cheers of their teammates and fans. The victory lap is not just a time to cool down after expending their maximum energy during the race, it's also time to pull together and move as one around the track in celebration of winning the race.

The same is true of the assimilation team at the church. Helping newcomers connect with Christ and the church in a profound and life-transforming way is cause for celebration. It is a time when all of the assimilation team efforts come together, and the newcomers are now ready to celebrate their faith in Jesus Christ and their belonging to the church by joining the church as members. Although the focus of assimilation has been on belonging, it is now time to help these connected newcomers join the church as an act of confirming and professing their faith in the living Christ.

ACTIVITY AND MEMBERSHIP

Membership is not the goal of assimilating new disciples; belonging, connecting, and being part of the church is our goal. It is our observation and conviction that too often the problem churches encounter in their assimilation process is focusing first on membership and then on assimilation. The problem with this sequence is that it often creates a large number of inactive members, because people tend to maintain the level of activity that they have at the time that they join for as long as they are a members. Granted, this is not universally true and there are noteworthy individual exceptions, but it is far more often true than not. Let's explore why through a couple of examples.

Let's say that someone attends your church twice in three months, is not involved in any spiritual formation groups or ministry teams, does not regularly contribute financially to the church, or help in any ministry. If this person joins the church and becomes a member, most often he or she will maintain that level of activity (or more accurately, inactivity) for as long as he or she is a member. In fact, as far as most of these inactive members are concerned, any additional involvement or participation is optional. Why? Pretty simple: if the church considered it important or central to being a member, it would have had the person do these things before becoming a member! Since the church didn't insist, and the person therefore didn't participate, all of these things are optional and the new member can do them, but they are not that important, let alone essential, to membership.

On the other hand, let's say someone else attends your church over three quarters of the time, is involved regularly in a Sunday school class or other study group, gives generously each week, and uses his or her spiritual gifts to actively engage in a ministry. When this person joins the church and becomes a member, most of the time he or she will continue to maintain this level of activity for as long as he or she is a member. Why? Pretty simple: these things seem essential to growing as a disciple and being a member, because your church helped this person to become active before joining. So fully assimilated newcomers are far more likely to be active, growing disciples of Jesus Christ and members of the church, than are those who join before they belong or are fully assimilated.

WHAT SYSTEMS PRODUCE

Lyle Schaller has stated: "Systems produce the outcomes they are designed to produce."[1] This principle describes why most mainline Protestant churches have significant numbers of inactive members. When the assimilation system is designed to produce members, many of them will be inactive because the system is not designed primarily to produce growing disciples for Jesus Christ. We would offer this corollary: "If systems produce what they are designed to produce and we are not satisfied with what is being produced, then instead of blaming the product, we need to change the system."

This principle and its corollary have obvious implications for how we design our system to assimilate new disciples. Too often in the church we get angry with inactive members. We get upset with them because they don't come to worship, don't participate in our classes and groups, don't help enough with the budget and expenses, and aren't involved in working with us in the ministries and programs of the church. We blame them because they are not more active. We fail to see our role in producing their inactivity by not connecting them with the church, not helping them belong before they joined. We taught them that coming occasionally to worship is good enough to join—and by extension, good enough as a follower of Jesus Christ. We developed the system that produced these inactive members, because we focused upon getting newcomers to join our membership, rather than focusing upon helping newcomers become assimilated as new disciples.

If we don't want to continue producing inactive members, then we need to change our system of discipleship and membership. Instead of encouraging membership with no effort on their part, we can have people join only after we have helped them to belong and to live out their discipleship in ways that help nourish their faith in Jesus Christ. There were four membership behaviors described above in both the active members (with positive examples of those behaviors) and inactive members (with negative examples of those same behaviors). What do those four behaviors have in common? For example, they are all part of the vows that members take when they join The United Methodist Church: "Will you be loyal to The United Methodist Church, and uphold it by your prayers [spiritual formation], your presence [worship attendance], your gifts [financial contributions], and your service [involvement in ministry]?"[2] Other denominations ask their members to take vows concerning similar behaviors. In other words, churches are asking the questions: Will we have newcomers live out their faith in these ways before they join? Will we be a church of higher expectations for members? Will we change the system from focusing upon membership to focusing upon discipleship? It is a key issue for all churches to decide. The church can change the system and invite persons to join after they demonstrate their discipleship by living these vows first, not perfectly but at least consistently.

Some will argue that setting a higher standard for membership closes off our open invitation to membership and seems more rooted in law than in grace. That may sound like a legitimate theological concern, but our theological perspective is that the primary task of the church is to help persons become disciples of Jesus Christ, not simply to add members, especially inactive members, to our church rolls. All newcomers are welcome to worship, pray, participate in spiritual growth groups and experiences, give generously as a response to God's grace, and use their gifts in ministry—all the things disciples are called and expected to do. It is this involvement in the life of the congregation that leads newcomers to be ready for membership. Some newcomers will even ask about becoming members. At such point they should not be discouraged from becoming members, but the church should share its expectations of membership and help them grow in their faith and discipleship toward those expectations. Providing such clarity about the meaning and expectations of membership is a more honest, hospitable, and helpful response. It should be a policy, with the full support of the church council, that we have high expectations of our membership and we are becoming a high-expectation church. It should become official policy that we help newcomers become assimilated and then we invite them to membership after they are already living out the vows of membership. Systems produce what they are designed to produce, and our calling is to produce disciples of Jesus Christ who become active, growing, involved, dedicated, committed, serving members.

MEMBERSHIP CLASSES

Another part of our system that encourages nonactive membership is the way we design our membership classes. The key question to ask as you consider the membership classes is this: "What kind of members do we want to develop?" In other words, it is helpful to use Stephen Covey's principle from *The Seven Habits of Highly Effective People* and "begin with the end in mind."[3] Picture first the way you hope the members of the church will behave and then develop the classes to reinforce and encourage this style and expectation. If our goal is to have members who are continuously growing as disciples of Jesus Christ, then the membership classes will focus on those resources and behaviors that will assist and express their growing discipleship. What would such a membership class design look like?

The first session of the membership classes (each of which might be sixty to ninety minutes) could focus on each new member's spiritual journey. All new members are given a chance to share a bit of their spiritual journey, centering on when they were closest to God, when they felt most distant, and what has helped them grow in their spiritual life. The leader of the class can also share his own faith journey, to set a pattern of sharing one's faith story. One of the keys to continuing to grow in our faith is for us to learn how to share our faith in a setting where others give us support and accountability on the spiritual journey. So the membership classes model this continuing lifelong practice. This first session also gives opportunity to affirm how the new members can be intentional about their spiritual growth and the things they are doing to assist that growth. The leader also shares opportunities within the life of the church to help with each person's spiritual journey—worship, small groups, Sunday school classes, Bible studies, covenant groups, share groups, prayer groups, communion, spiritual friendships and directors, and so forth. Session one affirms and encourages the centrality of spiritual growth for the new members as lifelong disciples of Jesus Christ.

The second session could be centered on Christian beliefs. At this session we would discuss the basics of the Christian faith, including topics such as God, Jesus Christ, the Holy Spirit, the church, and the Bible. This discussion would center on the questions of faith that the new members will be asked when they join the church. In this way, the liturgy of the membership vows forms the basis of the sharing together and affirmation of our Christian faith. This part of session two would vary based on one's denomination and theological tradition.

The third session could emphasize what it means to be a Christian from a particular denomination. For instance, learning what it means to be a United Methodist Christian, which has much in common with all Christians but some things that are unique. Among the more unique aspects of United Methodism, we would focus on history, doctrine, and polity. The history would be an overview of how the church has evolved into the church it is today. The polity would focus on the way the local church is organized for ministry (with a church council), appointments of pastors (through the bishop and district superintendents and the local church pastor-parish relations committee), and apportionments (shared mission as a church). The doctrinal discussion would look particularly at the sacraments of baptism (infants and adults) and communion as means of grace.

The fourth session could then address the meaning of membership. The session might begin by having the new members answer this question and share together their responses: "What do you expect of this church as a member?" The answers often include the basic and mundane (a heated building in the winter, cooling in the summer), to the practical and spiritual (care in the midst of crisis, education and spiritual growth opportunities for everyone in my family). Most of these could be affirmed as something the church could provide consistently to its members. And if there were expectations that our particular congregation could not provide (a strong singles group, a church orchestra), then those expectations could be identified so new members know that this is not available at the church and they would need to find it elsewhere, either by finding such a ministry in another church or by becoming a part of a church where that expectation could be met. The next question for all the new members to answer and then discuss together would be "What can the church expect of you as a member?" After a brief discussion together, we could then focus the discussion around a particular membership vow that centers on this vital issue. The discussion then gives the new members a chance to reflect and share together how they are already doing these things and how important these behaviors are for our continuing discipleship. This session might include the opportunity for the newcomers to do a spiritual gifts inventory (if this has not been done previously), with the chance to then dis-cuss the results with someone to help examine how to use those gifts in ministry.

Such a membership class design is intended to affirm disciple-ship and continuing growth in the very areas where the new members are already visibly living out their Christian faith. By helping persons belong and be connected to Christ and the church before they join, we are enabling the entire church to par-ticipate in the victory celebration once the relay race is com-plete.

YOUTH CONFIRMATION

Many churches struggle with the process of helping youth become members of the church through their participation in confirmation classes. Too many churches experience youth going through confirmation classes and then dropping out of active involvement in the life of the church after confirmation is fin-ished and they become members. It is frustrating to put signifi-cant energy and care into confirmation and to see so few transforming results in the lives of these youth. Is there a better process?

Indeed, there are processes that have a different and more pos-itive impact on the confirmands who participate. Systems pro-duce what they are designed to produce, and if the confirmation "system" is one that centers primarily on a classroom-style, information-imparting model, then it often produces young per-sons who "graduate" at the time they join the church as members and get their certificate of membership (which for many is the "diploma"). This is certainly not intended, but it is what the con-firmation system produces because that is what it is designed to produce.

If we want a different result, then we might want to seriously explore using a different process rather than blaming the confirmands (the "product") for not becoming more active, more connected, and more committed. Again it is helpful to ask the end-result question, "What kind of confirmands do we want to develop?" We can start with the end in mind and design a confirmation process to help these results to occur.

If we want to develop confirmands who are growing spiritually, connected relationally in their spiritual journey, examining their faith in a way that helps deal with their questions and concerns, developing healthy stewardship of resources and spiritual gifts, and involved in ministry using those gifts, then this will help guide us designing the confirmation experience. So rather than confirmation being an information/classroom/graduation/member process, we might focus on designing confirmation as a formation/experiential/mentor/disciple process instead. As we consider models for confirmation, we ought to realize that the generation we are seeking to disciple through confirmation is a "postmodern generation." As Leonard Sweet observes in his book *Post-modern Pilgrims*, it is important to design ministry that conforms to that culture he describes with the acronym E-P-I-C— Experientially, Participatory, Image-Driven, and Connected.[4]

A key to confirmation that disciples youth is the use of what are often called "faith guides," adults who participate with a particular confirmand throughout the process. They come to all the sessions, meet regularly with their confirmands for spiritual reflection on their devotional Bible readings and journaling, share in the projects, and become a spiritual friend and mentor in the faith. These persons are recruited from a list of several, active adults in the church that is submitted by each confirmand. This list of potential faith guides is developed by the confirmand in response to the question "What five adults who are active in this church (at least three of whom are not directly involved in youth ministry) live out their Christian faith in ways that you would like to follow?" So faith guides are persons who are already living out their faith in Jesus Christ in a way that the confirmand wants to emulate. (Such a process also makes recruiting faith guides easy! You simply tell the adult that a youth has identified her or him as someone whose faith the youth wants to emulate, and those adults can't help saying yes to becoming faith guides.) This faith guide model is helpful to the confirmation process because the Christian faith is caught more than simply taught.

Another key component of effective confirmation is helping the youth to experience the faith, and not just read or talk about it. The readings (and there are always some in confirmation) then come alive through experiential learning. This might include a faith walk (confirmands and faith guides pairing up and trading off leading the other blindfolded) and then reflecting on the experience of trust and how it was true for the persons of faith in the Bible, like Abraham. It might be discovering spiritual gifts of the confirmand and faith guide—and using them to develop a service ministry of four or more total hours—along with reflecting and sharing with the other confirmands and faith guides the meaning of their experiences as disciples. The confirmand and faith guide might attend an administrative meeting and a program area meeting and share what they learned about the nature of ministry in the church. The team of confirmand and faith guide might reflect on a worship service together. They might also read together the confirmation materials about doctrines and develop questions to share with the pastor for discussions and discovery learning. The sessions will certainly need to include visuals to make relevant what is being shared with the confirmands. In this model, the ten to twelve sessions (2 to 2½ hours long once a month) are highly participatory, image-driven and experiential, requiring confirmands to connect with one another, with their faith guide, and with Jesus Christ.

The confirmation process builds toward Confirmation Sunday, the high point of a faith-transforming process. This worship service is planned and led by the confirmands—the prayers, the affirmation of faith, the selection of the music, the children's sermon. The sermon by the pastor should be a message especially for the confirmands, with the congregation free to overhear. Their faith guide, parents, and church leaders could confirm each youth, with laying on of hands. Oftentimes the service will include communion—with the team of confirmand and faith guide helping to serve the elements.

What we have outlined here is a process that focuses on discipling and spiritual growth, done in E-P-I-C style! And what is the result? Most confirmands continue to be active disciples in the church, having been connected with the church and its ministry, and with Jesus Christ, through the vital relationship with the faith guide. These confirmands do not tend to graduate from their classroom time of informing; instead they tend to stay connected and continue to be formed as disciples with their spiritual mentors. It is true—systems produce what they are designed to produce, whether for youth or adults. And the culmination of belonging, connecting, and discipling is joining. It is indeed a celebration of a victory lap in the relay race of assimilation.

OTHER GENERATIONAL ISSUES

These same principles apply to another generational issue facing most churches as they seek to develop an assimilation process that leads toward active membership: attracting young adults from Generation X. Pastors and lay leaders often comment, "Young adults today just don't want to make a commitment to join an institution like the church." While there is some truth to statements like that, such statements often become an excuse or rationalization for not seeking ways to involve and include young adults into full discipleship and church membership.

It is true that those in what is often termed Generation X (generally considered to be those born between 1964 and 1982) are not guided by the same kind of institutional loyalty, respect for hierarchy, and response to calls for sacrifice, as were previous generations. Gen-Xers especially, are motivated by quite different factors than the "Silent Generation" (those born before 1946),[5] who are often the ones in our churches who complain, "Those young adults are just not as committed to the church as they should be!"

So how do we in the church provide a system that attracts Gen-Xers to become members? Our focus upon belonging before joining is the answer. Young adults are not likely to join an institution; however, they are attracted to relationships and causes that make a difference in their lives. When inviting young adults to consider becoming members of our churches, it is crucial to focus upon helping their journey toward discipleship rather than focusing upon the church's desire to increase its membership. Young adults today (Gen-Xers and the emerging new generation often called Generation Y or the Millennial Generation) are not attracted to churches whose primary focus is upon the church's survival as an institution. However, young adults are attracted to churches that honestly invite, welcome, respond to, and include them in a journey of faith that makes a difference in their lives.

CONCLUSION

Very few of us would enter into a wedding with someone who was unwilling to listen to us, did not respect us or our opinion, was not sensitive or caring, did not allow us to participate in the decision making, or refused to stand by us in difficulty or stress. Few of us would believe that, once the vows were pronounced and we were finally married, our spouse would now magically and wonderfully turn a sharp 180 degrees and now become attentive, listening, responsive, respectful, caring, open, willing to share in decision making, and supportive regardless of the circumstances. Why? Because we want to see those behaviors consistently and genuinely before the wedding, so we know that they are central in our relationship. The vows are an affirmation and confirmation of what is already true in our relationship.

The same can be true of membership vows. Rather than hoping that persons who are not involved in intentional spiritual formation, attend worship very sporadically, contribute rarely, and do not help in ministry will somehow magically turn around that behavior with the recitation of the membership vows, we need to see persons coming to membership having already lived out the vows of membership in their faith journey in prayers, presence, gifts, and service. The vows are an affirmation and confirmation of what is already true in our relationship with Jesus Christ and the church. Systems produce what they are designed to produce. May the system of newcomer assimilation and membership in your church produce vital, growing, active disciples of Jesus Christ who are also dedicated, involved, and serving members of the church to which you belong.

* * *

As the Newcomers Team members gathered for their regular Monday morning meeting, they were all discussing the previous day's worship service. "It was such a nice celebration!" said Susie. "I was thrilled to see Jennifer standing there, looking so proud of her young children, obviously feeling at home in our church, and taking her membership vows."

"For me, the biggest thrill," said Jill, "was seeing Cathy step out of the women's ensemble group where she is so involved, join her husband, Bill, and smile so beautifully as she joined our church. Knowing a little of what she has been through with this move to town and all, it was just a privilege to know that we had all been a part of helping both of them belong and then join our church."

The discussion continued, and finally the group turned to their new list of first-time newcomers to start the assimilation process with those persons. On their list today was the name Sarah Johnson, who apparently was Bill and Cathy's daughter. "I know that she may have just come on Sunday to be with her parents when they joined," Clyde said, "but when Norma and I visited with her during the reception for newcomers, I sensed that she might also be a seeker. I hope that we will not overlook her, because being here with her parents might have been her way of tiptoeing into our church looking for answers." Clyde's reminder was well received, and the team made plans to call her and look for future opportunities to invite her to participate. "Who knows?" Jill said. "Maybe Jennifer will be a contact person to help connect with her. I noticed that those two young women were really talking during the reception time."

"*Speaking of Jennifer,*" said Norma, "*did you meet that lovely couple who run the coffee shop where she works? It must have meant so much to Jennifer to have them come to church for her membership Sunday. Do you think Jennifer invited them? Do you think they might be more than just visitors?*" Norma's rapid questions led to more plans to welcome, respond, and invite.

Steve surprised the group with another interesting connection on their list of first-time visitors. "*I had a great conversation with Kareem Thomas and his wife, Lateesha. He told me that Bill has been helping him through the SCORE program—you know, getting his business started—and Bill invited them to come to church yesterday. How's that for new members reaching out to the community, inviting others, and living out their discipleship? Let's not forget to respond to Kareem and his family.*"

And so Newcomers Team members developed plans for their latest list of newcomers, and the assimilation relay race continued.

1. ATTRACTING NEWCOMERS

1. Lyle Schaller, *Survival Tactics in the Parish* (Nashville: Abingdon Press, 1997), 118. Adobe Reader e-book.
2. Many books on marketing have noted the concept of the stages of readiness, including *Marketing for Nonprofit Organizations* by Philip Kotler (Englewood Cliffs, N.J.: Prentice-Hall, 1975).
3. George Gallup Jr., *The Unchurched American* (Princeton, N.J.: Princeton Religious Research Center, 1978).
4. Two specific studies have looked at this issue: Michael J. Coyner's "Why People Join" (doctoral research project, Drew University, October 1, 1980) found 100 percent of new members had a "precipitant event"; and Dean R. Hoge et al., *Converts, Dropouts, Returnees: A Study of Religious Change Among Catholics* (Washington, D.C.: United States Catholic Conference; New York: Pilgrim Press, 1981), which studied two hundred Roman Catholic parishes and found 97 percent of all new converts had "facilitating events" that prompted their movement toward a parish.

2. WELCOMING NEWCOMERS

1. Henri Nouwen, *Reaching Out* (Garden City, N.Y.: Doubleday, 1975), 63-110.
2. See Genesis 18.
3. This phrase has been developed by Douglas Anderson to summarize the results of his research about newcomers and the ways in which they are helped to feel welcome. His unpublished doctoral study, "Hospitable Worship as Evangelism" (Drew University, October 1, 1980) includes the discovery that 80

percent of the issues named by newcomers that helped them to feel welcome at a church occurred before the actual worship service began.

4. Lyle Schaller, *44 Questions for Congregational Self-Appraisal* (Nashville: Abingdon Press, 1998), 75.

5. Tom Peters describes this syndrome in *A Passion for Excellence* by Tom Peters and Nancy Austin (New York: Random House, 1985).

6. Douglas Anderson, "Welcome to Worship: We Speak Your Language," *Your Church* (March/April 1983): 37-45.

7. Margaret Wheatley, *Leadership and the New Science*, 2nd ed. (San Francisco: Berrett-Koehler, 1994), 49-52.

4. RESPONDING TO NEWCOMERS

1. Herb Miller, *Fishing on the Asphalt: Effective Evangelism in Mainline Denominations* (St. Louis: Bethany Press, 1983). The phrase about the "3 Be's" comes from Miller's seminars.

5. LISTENING TO NEWCOMERS

1. Dean Hoge et al., *Converts, Dropouts, Returnees: A Study of Religious Change Among Catholics* (Washington, D.C.: United States Catholic Conference; New York: Pilgrim Press, 1981).

2. Michael J. Coyner, "Why People Join" (doctoral research project, Drew University, October 1, 1980).

6. INCLUDING NEWCOMERS

1. Stephen R. Covey, *The Seven Habits of Highly Effective People: Restoring the Character Ethic* (New York: Simon and Schuster, 1989), 95.

2. Leonard I. Sweet, *Post-modern Pilgrims: First Century Passion for the 21st Century World* (Nashville: Broadman & Holman, 2000).

3. Philip G. Zimbardo, *Shyness: What It Is, What to Do About It* (Cambridge, Mass.: Perseus Books, 1989), 14.

7. INCLUDING NEWCOMERS AS NEW MEMBERS

1. Lyle Schaller, *From Geography to Affinity* (Nashville: Abingdon Press, 2003), 25.
2. *The United Methodist Book of Worship* (Nashville: The United Methodist Publishing House, 1992), 109.
3. Stephen R. Covey, *The Seven Habits of Highly Effective People: Restoring the Character Ethic* (New York: Simon and Schuster, 1989), 95.
4. Leonard I. Sweet, *Post-modern Pilgrims: First Century Passion for the 21st Century World* (Nashville: Broadman & Holman, 2000), xxi.
5. Many books speak to the issue of generational differences. Among those most helpful are *Generations at Work* by Ron Zemke, Claire Raines, and Bob Filipczak (New York: Amacom, 2000) and *Millennials Rising* by Neil Howe and Bill Strauss (New York: Vintage Books, 2000).